PRAISE

"In *Tending Your Roots*, Mindi offers readers a transformative journey, unpacking personal, ancestral, and collective trauma and illuminating the interconnectedness between us humans, our ancestors, and the Earth. Drawing from traditional wisdom and modern science, Mindi guides readers with compassion, empowering them to confront and tend to deep-seated wounds. Through her heartfelt approach and commitment to global healing, she inspires readers to reclaim agency in their healing journey, fostering resilience and connection between the inner and outer landscapes. This book serves as a beacon of hope, offering a timeless roadmap to wholeness and healing amidst life's challenges."

—Dr. Arielle Schwartz, Clinical Psychologist and author of *The Post-Traumatic Growth Guidebook* and *The Complex PTSD Workbook* and founder of The Center for Resilience Informed Therapy

"This offering and guidebook presents a gentle, grounded, and well-informed set of tools and teachings for not just transforming trauma but coming back into conscious relationship with the rest of life. In this way, Mindi Counts gets to the heart of the matter by providing tangible ways to transition from cultural isolation into a greater sense of belonging, responsibility, and Earth reconnection."

—Daniel Foor, Ph.D., author of *Ancestral Medicine: Rituals for Personal and Family Healing*

"A clear and compassionate guide to becoming whole again, *Tending Your Roots* is an access-point to understand more about yourself and your belonging through reconnecting with the sentience of the living world. Highlighting the connection between trauma healing, attachment wounds, and our own relationship with the Earth, Mindi brings forth a vitally missing piece to the Western world's understanding of wellbeing–and opens a gateway for profound healing. With practical exercises and pathways, Mindi illuminates the way forward in a grounded, care-filled, and gentle way. Like a sit spot in nature, dwelling in the field of this book is a healing experience unto itself."

—Asia Suler, author of *Mirrors in the Earth:*
Reflections on Healing from the Living World

TENDING
—*Your*—
ROOTS

AN EARTH-CENTERED APPROACH TO HEALING
PERSONAL, ANCESTRAL, AND COLLECTIVE TRAUMA

MINDI K. COUNTS MA, LAC

Author: Mindi K. Counts MA, LAC.
Website: mindikcounts.com
Tending Your Roots/ Mindi K. Counts MA, LAC. First edition.
Publisher: MKC Creative

ISBN: 979-8-9897441-0-7 (paperback), 979-8-9897441-1-4(hardcover).

To all who fear their wounds are too old and too deep
to heal, I dedicate this book especially to you

CONTENTS

Acknowledgments...xi

Preface..1

Introduction 5

Opening 10

PART ONE: A WOUNDED WORLD

Chapter One: Our Inner and Outer Landscapes 15

Chapter Two: Trauma Living in Our Nervous Systems...................25

Chapter Three: Our Hunter-Gatherer Sensory Systems 49

Chapter Four: Boundaries as an Essential Survival Skill.................63

PART TWO: PERSONAL, ANCESTRAL, AND COLLECTIVE TRAUMA

Chapter Five: Personal Trauma and Attachment Wounds 89

Chapter Six: Ancestral Trauma...115

Chapter Seven: Collective Trauma 131

Chapter Eight: Original Trauma.......................................147

PART THREE: YOU ARE NOT SEPARATE

Chapter Nine: Establishing Your Secure Base 165

Chapter Ten: Discovering Your Plant Allies 171

Chapter Eleven: Welcoming Animals as Teacher 181

Chapter Twelve: Connecting with a Healthy Ancestor 189

Chapter Thirteen: Entering the Wilderness 195

Afterword.. 221

End Notes 227

Resources.. 233

OFFERING

As a fellow human on the healing journey, I'd like to welcome you into my world with a special invitation. Please visit mindikcounts.com/offerings/tendingyourroots for exclusive access to join a community of kindred souls who also long to live in a gentler, more connected world and with greater access to healing resources. In this space, you will find offerings that include downloadable meditations, guides, and sacred practices to accompany you on your journey through *Tending Your Roots*.

ACKNOWLEDGMENTS

MANY YEARS AGO when I began writing *Tending Your Roots,* I soon realized and shared with my partner, "This book will be the death of me." If you are a creator, artist, and/or a passionate being on a mission—then you will understand what I meant. And if, as this book makes its way to you it turns out that I was correct, I want you to know that I am survived by so many amazing support people who encouraged, loved, challenged, and pushed me in a myriad of ways of which I can never fully express my gratitude.

To start I want to acknowledge Marlow, my 'Grandmother of the West' who first taught me to listen to my nervous system and trust that there was wisdom to the anxiety and grief I had been carrying all my life. And who— over the course of decades, welcomed me into the world of real and deep plant friendships. Without her guidance and wisdom, I likely would not have found the courage to listen to my own authentic voice and to step so fiercely into the expansive healing terrain. She is a reminder that—sometimes, all it takes is one person to truly believe in you.

I then want to acknowledge the wild woman with blue feathers in her hair whose name I will never know but who randomly pulled a tarot card for me at a festival as I was driving through this tiny mountain town and declared, "you need to stop everything you are doing and return to your first passion: writing."

Appreciating her unsolicited forwardness, I wound up calling my friend some months later who is an astrologer and asked him to look into my chart to confirm if this information had any credence. He indeed saw writing, teaching, and communication was a massive part of my North Node, a.k.a. my evolution during this lifetime. Thank you for your trust in the stars, Adam.

After that, I want to acknowledge my late four-legged rescue, Gemma Sue who if it weren't for her timidity and clumsiness she would never have gotten her leash wrapped around the sandwich board sign that knocked over during our morning walk and revealed, "Unleash Your Inner Author, A Budding Writer's Workshop" and then I never would have met Amy, a woman who saw something in me I couldn't see in myself at the time. A woman who ultimately became my writing coach and cheerleader for many years and many manuscripts to come.

Juree and Jennifer, best friends and editors for Shambhala Publications—saw potential in me to shed light on and bring clarity into the world of holistic healing literature and helped me land my first book deal for *Everyday Chinese Medicine: Healing Remedies for Immunity, Vitality, and Optimal Health*. A deep bow to you both.

With permission from my loved ones, my plant allies, my animal teachers—and the clear but often forceful nudges from the Universe, I set sail and began writing almost every morning. Thanks to my growing network of resources and support, I trusted I was on the right path.

Since then, there have been countless people who have supported me in this journey, who have swam with me in the dark waters of doubt, and who have celebrated the mini-milestones that naturally come along with the creative process, even when they feel insignificant. My partner, Jonathan takes the cake on this one. He was the first to listen to my tales of the wild woman in the mountains and the astrology reading and the story of our Gemma Sue, dropping a fifty-dollar bill into my "Reality Fund" jar to help make my dreams come true. I still have the fifty, and I still have the jar. Thank you for being the first to believe in me as an artist, writer and creator.

Andrea, Jen, Kristen, Becca, Amanda, Kristi, Chris, and Katie are among just a few of the friendships that experienced some or all of the following: long delays in communication, canceled plans, last minute requests to review something, and otherwise co-holding with me—the paradoxical joy and burden of the creative process. I hold my hand over my heart, my chin quivering, and I bow deeply to you (and ask for forgiveness from you), my soul-friends. I love and cherish each of you and all the ways that you have been flexible without warning and sacrificed for this book. Thank you, thank you.

To Jaki, our beloved au pair from Argentina who has been my right hand (and also sometimes left), tag-teaming my spirited daughter with me during the final stages of birthing this manuscript. I could not have focused long enough to complete this without your presence, your love, and care for our daughter and family. Desde el fondo de mi corazón, gracias.

To my four-leggeds, past and present, thank you for all the cuddles, your flexibility in the timing of our neighborhood walks, and the dead weight on my legs as you dreamt of adventure while I sat writing obsessively on the couch. I hope to make it up to you in this lifetime or the next.

To all those who came before me, seen and unseen—who cheer me on from the other side. To those who drop feathers in my path when it's time for me to lift my gaze and remind me of who I am, where I come from, and that I belong to this world. Though I may never see you or squeeze you, I know you are there and your presence fills me with courage.

And last but not least, thank you to Mother Earth for being my rock—literally and metaphorically. I would not be here without you and your magnificent creation. I would not have been able to tend the roots of my own traumas, the traumas of my ancestors, or the collective traumas of which I am inevitably intertwined. Thank you for your patience with me and for letting me witness just a little bit of your magic. I do not take you for granted.

For anyone I missed, please know that the brain of someone who just completed a manuscript is unreliable at best and needs time to rest. Much like how a new baby yields a necessary postpartum period, having birthed a new book requires a similar healing process: warm, nutrient dense broths, frequent naps, and a few dear friends to drop by here and there for a visit to hold this new little being in their arms and say, "awwww." Know that I still love you.

PREFACE

LET ME START BY INTRODUCING MYSELF: I am a woman who has worked through layers of trauma—childhood, ancestral, and intergenerational—to arrive at a healthy and connected place where I feel deeply rooted in my body, resilient, and with an unshakeable sense of belonging to the Earth. In this book, I share my journey so that you can discover the possibility of repatterning your own nervous system and the consequential healing that is your birthright.

I was born on this Earth as a Southern, white-bodied, cis-gendered woman, and from a lineage of European colonizers who landed in Virginia and North Carolina in the 1700s in Powhatan and Manahoac territories. We were immigrants from Denmark, England, Ireland, and Scotland, having survived a shipwreck off the coast of Prince Edward Island, where our lives were saved by the Indigenous Mi'kmaq people. We lived on P.E.I. for many years before making our way to Suffolk County (modern-day Boston area), and then eventually to the southern states, which I called home as a child.

I was raised in a blue-collar, working-class family always on the brink of poverty. Looking back, it is obvious to me now that there was significant residue of trauma living in our lineage that reared its head in our family system through drug and alcohol addiction, violence, suicide, anxiety, depression,

PTSD, and various degrees of abuse. I was able to unearth the courage needed to leave home and emancipate when I was sixteen, becoming the first in my family to go to college and forge a new path for my lineage. Stories like mine are rare. It is not easy to fall so far from the family tree.

The pervasive effects of trauma and tangible lack of belonging within my family of origin, compounded by the programming of scarcity, fear, and hyper-individualism in my culture, is what has led me on my own journey of deep and dangerous healing, trauma-tending, and of ultimately finding where I belong. From there, I have created an unapologetically authentic and meaningful life. I imagine you are here because you too, have struggled in familiar terrain and long for similar things.

My background as a healer is varied. As a child, I always knew I wanted to be a therapist of sorts. However, after seeing the limitations in the "us and them" paradigm that lives at the core of much of Western psychology, I knew it wasn't for me. After a two-year immersion in traditional academia, I followed my intuition and left the program for a Buddhist-inspired university, earning a degree in contemplative psychology where the approach is that *we are not separate*. This rare lens through which to view psychology, led by the wisdom teachings of Chogyam Trungpa Rinpoche, is what gave me the confidence to trust myself enough to step out of my comfort zone and sign up for experiences such as multi-week-long silent retreats deep in the mountains, where all you have is your own mind and body to contend with. Eventually, I had the courage to sign up for the first of what would become countless solo excursions into the wilderness to explore my psyche and personal relationship with the Earth and her beings.

Longing to understand this powerful influence the Earth and her beings have on me (and all of us) led me to study ecopsychology and soak up the teachings of Joanna Macy and Bill Plotkin, as well as Depth and Jungian psychology and the teachings of Dr. Clarissa Pinkola Estes. I took a deep dive into the trauma-focused work of Bessel van der Kolk, Dan Siegel, Peter Levine, and the body of wisdom known as Somatic Experiencing. I have also studied shamanism, animism, and Earth-based ways of healing with Indigenous elders from the Lakota lineage, the Huichol lineage, and various lineages of the Himalayas. I kept tracing the history of this ecopsychological paradigm farther and farther back, eventually winding up at the doors of Eastern philosophy, one of the oldest documented Earth-based systems of healing. In 2012, I graduated with a master's degree in Classical Five Element Chinese Medicine and started a private practice while simultaneously beginning my work with Indigenous communities in India, Nepal, Thailand, and Burma. Daily, I am influenced by the wisdom and fortitude of my patients, students, and fellow colleagues traversing the trauma terrain for the sake of greater healing, helping us remember where we have come from, that we are not separate, and working to create a more balanced and just world with room for us all.

The power of being immersed in the natural world, away from the influence of Western culture, was the first place in my life where I truly felt free, where I could feel my heartbeat and hear my own unadulterated voice. And it was there, deep in the woods, where I felt for the first time the extraordinarily powerful medicine of Mother Earth and her capacity to repattern my nervous system out of a state of trauma, and into a state of wellness, resilience, and with a sense of deep belonging. I invite you to journey along with me so that you can learn to do the same with yours.

In this book, I share my stories, experiences, and all that has guided and supported me on my path of transformation out of a state of trauma. I have no intention of teaching you how to be me, even though I know the importance of being inspired by and leaning on others while you carve out and uncover your own path. Ultimately, I want to support you in becoming more fully you as a rooted, embodied, deeply compassionate, well-bounded, and powerful being who knows without a doubt that you belong to the Earth. Therefore, if you read things in this book that don't feel aligned right now at this moment—let them go. Please take only what fits for you and keep moving through.

I recognize that my voice, privilege, stories, and insights cannot possibly meet every soul who reads these pages. Therefore, I invite you into my world with the awareness that my particular lens will be coloring the stories and experiences I share with you. I am—like you—attempting to wake up in our often challenging world, and I most certainly have my blind spots. I may make some generalizations that don't align with your personal or cultural experiences or both. Your reactions to this are valid and important to me. I hope that the following stories and insights will land in the hands of those who most need to hear them, along with those also willing to examine and tease apart how their world is uniquely colored. The path of tending your roots and repatterning your nervous system for wellness and belonging is, after all, a path of honing in on our truth and honoring both the brilliance and shadow of our shared humanness.

Living now in the occupied, unceded Ute, Arapaho, and Cheyenne territories, otherwise known as Colorado, I am influenced daily by the spirits of this land. I care a lot about the world we live in and have devoted my life to service. On behalf of the Earth, and the plants and animals who are and have always been speaking to us—it is time for us to listen . . . .

Thank you for trusting me to accompany you on your journey. I do not take it lightly.

Much love and many wild blessings,
Mindi

INTRODUCTION:

YOU ARE NOT SEPARATE.

You Belong Here. This World Needs You.

MOST OF US SPEND OUR DAYS knowing something is deeply out of alignment. We are moving much too fast for our bodies, psyches, and spirits. We feel as though we are at the mercy of our lives. We are sick, sad, anxious, afraid, and lonely. And we feel separate from other humans, plants, animals, and the Earth herself. If you have unhealed trauma, if you are burned out, moving too fast, taking on too much, valuing yourself by your productivity, and have lost touch with your deep inner landscape and the ripe, timely wisdom contained within, this book is for you.

With the support of the Earth, we all have the ability to tend to our past traumas and heal from the wounds we carry both inside ourselves and out into the world. It is time for us to wake from our slumber, come out of our trauma responses, and offer ourselves the gift of healing by partnering with the Earth, our greatest resource and ally. When you choose to do this work, it will become the most powerful homecoming of your life.

This book is an invitation to awaken and repattern your nervous system for authenticity, wellness, and belonging, despite the challenges you have experienced on your journey. With this part of you awakened, you will *embody*. You will once again learn to trust your own instincts and heart to instruct and guide you. You will become more fully rooted and in constant conversation with the Earth. With her support, your healing journey will bring you the deep medicine you have been longing for. This medicine lives inside of you already and its power lies in your connection to and relationship with your body, the Earth, and her elements—water, wood, fire, earth, and metal, as well as her flora and fauna.

To heal requires work. With my guidance, I invite you to tend to *your* roots, starting with focusing inward toward your own wounding and unmet needs; you'll then explore the trauma passed on from your family and past generations, and finally the trauma of the land and from disconnecting from the Earth—what I refer to as the *original trauma*. Once you arrive here, you will be invited to fully and unwaveringly root yourself back into the Earth with a nervous system that has been repatterned out of a state of trauma and into a state of healing.

The healing journey I present in this book can be taken over the course of one cycle of seasons or many. The choice is yours—and that of your nervous system's ability—to track and integrate the work we are about to do. I have included several invitations to expand your awareness, strengthen your connection to your body and to the body of the Earth, deepen your relationship with the Earth and her beings, and work diligently, however slowly, toward healing, homing, and belonging.

It takes time to unlearn harmful ways of being in our bodies and on the Earth. It also takes time to repattern our psyches for goodness and love. It takes time to integrate healing. I have written this book holding this awareness front and center; so that you can return to these pages, again and again, at different phases of your healing journey and at different times in your life. I recommend reading this book cover to cover and pausing to make space for a practice when you feel a resonance with the invitation. I share these invitations to support your integration of the material. If we only read the material, we will digest it only on a mental level. Since our work together must include the body and nervous system, we must engage with the material at that level, too, so that we embody and ground the work in a way that changes our lives tangibly and does not rely on our memory of the material alone.

The Many Traumas That Require Tending

We've all witnessed or experienced trauma on one or many levels. To be human *is to experience trauma*. Let's take a look at this inner and outer landscape we find ourselves in and why this is happening.

The field of *ecopsychology*, the study and merging of the fields of ecology and psychology to better understand human-nature relationships, has reminded us again and again of the importance of our mental and physical health in relationship with the Earth. Research in this field such as the study of the mental health benefits of spending time each day in the natural world (1) or the study of nature-based activities and their life-changing effect on children with adverse childhood experiences (2), has unearthed the tremendously important connection between human mental health and the natural world. In his book, *Blinded by Science,* Matthew Silverstone shares the evidence that being with trees leads to substantial increases in oxytocin, which is the same hormone that your body produces during moments of emotional bonding.

I would venture to say that we are, in fact, *nature herself.* We are not separate from what we call the "natural world." We *are* the natural world. And inextricably woven into the Earth, the more separation we feel from the natural world through our psychological states and lifestyles, the ecopsychological lens proposes, the more dis-ease we will feel and the more mental and physical health problems will arise, both inside of us and also on the Earth. And we are seeing this dis-ease manifest as the rates of environmental crises and mental health crises skyrocket in tandem (3).

The Healing Journey

In the pages that follow, we will embark on a voyage together to witness, make sense of, and tend to the root of our trauma so that we can access our innate sense of belonging, beyond family lines and communities: our belonging to the Earth. On our voyage, I want to prepare you; there will be ups and downs; there will be uncharted territory and rocky terrain; there will be unexpected twists and turns, places where you will want to duck and run, and places where you will need to disrobe from all of your usual vices and dive into the deep waters of your inner landscape. I am taking you to these seemingly fraught places only out of my deep love—and concern for humanity. This is the work we, and the Earth, are literally *dying for*.

The work we are doing together in this book to tend to our traumas can be liberating—and also painful. Trauma has taught us that to remain safe, we must brace ourselves mentally and physically for any possibility of harm. However, if during our healing journey we don't stretch our physical and emotional muscles, they will remain in a contracted state. As we begin stretching our muscles by unpacking *how we got here,* we inevitably find a deep well of unmet needs, parts of ourselves that we wrote off long ago. I will provide tools for working directly with this throughout this book. I invite you to partake in the practices that will help you embody each stage on your healing journey. Through these practices, you will have an opportunity to tend to your traumas and to integrate healing moments along the way. These opportunities will also bring your body physically closer to the Earth so that you can become entrained with the very pulse of the Earth and your nervous system will naturally begin repatterning for wellness. You will find yourself with greater capacity for your life and with a deeper connection to yourself and others.

Learning to Do Things Differently

For you to become whole and healthy in your body and psyche, for you to become available to the full spectrum of your life, and to drink up the wisdom of your experiences, you *must* learn to do things differently now. Therefore, before we go any further on our journey, I'd love for you to name your intention for reading this book. Why did you pick it up? What are you hoping to gain? Perhaps you sense something in you is longing to be witnessed, to be tended to, and repaired. Setting an intention puts you back on the horse, the reins in your hands. You are no longer simply at the mercy of what is happening—you are now a full participant.

With your intention set, I need you to know something. I need the ancient, buried, raw, core part of you, who lives underneath all the doing, all the wounding, and all the fear, to hear a few things from me directly. While these messages are implicit throughout this entire book, in the interest of my deep desire to be of service to you, to walk alongside you and be your guide onto the path of tending to your unhealed trauma, I want to name these transmissions explicitly. Drink in these ideas now, before we go any further.

I realize that these are things that no one in your life has likely had the courage to tell you. I want to tell you what you knew the moment you were conceived, but you forgot because those around you forgot it for themselves, too. These ideas might be difficult to swallow at first because they will go against everything you have ever been taught. But if you can lean on me *and my trust in you* for the moment, I know you will be so glad you did. Here we go:

You are not separate. You belong here and this world needs you.

If you can open your heart to its capacity and engage with the material that follows, I promise you, you will make tremendous strides on your healing journey, and you will develop an untapped level of authenticity, belonging, and resilience that will carry you throughout the rest of your life.

Ready, steady—we have our work cut out for us. Since you have picked up this book, I know there is a fire lit inside of you; there is a part of you that is not sleepwalking, that is awake, and who knows *we are living out of alignment with our true selves.* That part lives in me, too. Tether yourself to that part for the time being, and let the healing journey unravel.

OPENING

The small plot of ground
on which you were born
cannot be expected

To stay forever
the same.
Earth changes,
and home becomes different
places.

You took flesh
from clay
but the clay
did not come
from just one
place.

To feel alive,
important, and safe,
know your own waters
and hills, but know
more.

You have stars in your bones
and oceans
in blood.

You have opposing terrain
in each eye
you belong to the land
and sky of your first cry,
you belong to infinity.

—Alla Rennee Bozarth

PART ONE:
A WOUNDED WORLD

"When we no longer know what to do, we have come to our real work and when we no longer know which way to go, we have begun our real journey."

—Wendell Berry

IN PART ONE, we will peer into the inner and outer landscapes so that we can witness and understand how they are inextricably interwoven and why we need to turn our attention toward both of them simultaneously if we are to tend to the root of our traumas. We will unpack what the possibility of *health* looks like in our world, as well as how trauma and trauma responses appear. We will hold space as we become familiar with the ways in which these two collide and impact one another. And we will enter into the first of many invitations to practice skills that will not only support us on our healing journey, but they will also support our development of capacity and resilience to the unique challenges our modern world presents.

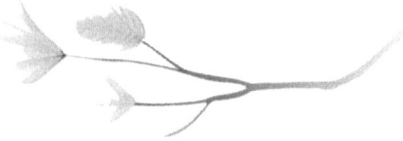

CHAPTER ONE:

OUR INNER AND OUTER LANDSCAPES

IF, LIKE ME, YOU LONG TO LIVE A LIFE with greater authenticity, an unshakeable sense of belonging, and a deep well of resilience, you must first examine and tease apart trauma, yours and the traumas of those close to you and in your family lineage, to see how it has shaped your psyche and patterned your nervous system. The more you witness the threads that connect your traumas to the complex and often chaotic world you—and all of us, have found ourselves in, the more capacity you will grow for your own life, no matter the terrain.

By *belonging,* I am referring to an intrinsic state of feeling at home inside yourself that is not influenced by changing outside factors. Imagine for a moment what that might feel like. How different would your life look if this was your homeostasis?

Before I go on, let's talk about what *health* looks like. Health is not the absence of suffering. Health is rather the capacity to hold who we are at the center of our beings, even while we are suffering. It is that ability to sway far and wide as our lives require—even into unbelievably painful terrain at times—and yet return to our center, over and over again. Health is feeling safe inside of ourselves. Health is trusting ourselves and having compassion for our survival strategies. Health stems from a deep knowing that we are connected to the Earth, that we belong, and that we can straddle possibility alongside our grief. When we feel we belong, it affirms who we are from inside ourselves and we feel more welcome to express that which is authentic to us. Having some sense of who you are and what you value, having trust in your natural impulses, and being anchored in your integrity *is health*. Health is accessible to all of us, no matter how sick you think or fear you have become. Health is the by-product of finding home inside yourself and yet is fully interdependent with the physical and emotional environment of our outer landscape.

Healing the Outer Landscape

In our high-tech modern world we have not been kind to the Earth; we have treated her resources as objects for us to use when needed and discard when finished. We destroy wild places in exchange for cookie-cutter neighborhoods and landscaped greenery. We build fences and gates and destroy the very ecosystems that make a place unique and beautiful just so that we can build more homes to manage the ever-increasing population or build more retail stores so that we can consume beyond our wildest dreams. For centuries, we have been exploiting Earth's resources. Our addiction to fossil fuels has led to global warming that challenges any and all life on Earth.

Seventy-five percent of land on Earth is considered significantly degraded, and despite growing awareness of this rapid and expansive degradation, it hasn't stopped or even slowed down. Each hour, 1,692 acres of productive dry land becomes desert due to continued deforestation (1). Simultaneously, in the US alone, more than 20 percent of our population has been diagnosed with mental illness, and more than 50 percent of our population in the US suffers from chronic illness (2).

Healing the Inner Landscape

What we do to the Earth and to each other is simply a mirror to what is happening inside ourselves. We are isolated and lonely. We feel separate. Many of us feel as though we don't belong, not in our communities, our families, or even inside our own skin.

In the US, we are dealing with unprecedented rates of health problems, insulin resistance, cancer, and diabetes. Our digestive systems aren't functioning properly as we are relying on so much processed food to sustain us; food that has been tainted with pesticides and other chemicals. While there have been many incredible advances in Western medicine (especially emergency medicine), such as the invention of antibiotics, our microbiomes are now becoming fragile from their overuse. Rates of chronic illness are astronomical, as well as thyroid imbalances, infertility, and autoimmune conditions. Heart disease is rampant, as is high cholesterol. Each day we are dealing with toxins from the air we breathe, the food we eat, and the water we drink. We ingest toxins at a rate greater than what we are able to process and detoxify from our bodies, leading to all kinds of diseases and nutritional deficiencies. We are inflamed, our bodies are exhausted, and with our limited time and resources to attempt to get our needs met, most of us teeter on the edge of addiction from screens to substances, just to get through each day.

What is happening to our bodies is simply an outward expression of what is happening to our minds. We are anxious and depressed. Some of us are even still tackling life at full speed while dealing with anxiety and depression leading to a relatively new psychological diagnosis called *high-functioning depression*. High-functioning depression is easily overlooked as its hallmark symptom is to be high-functioning, something that is rewarded in our Western society. Yet, just underneath the surface lies fear, hopelessness, and the longing to withdraw.

In our fear of failure, we are becoming perfectionists and attempting to control anything we can get our hands on. Many of us have developed appeasing behaviors just to get by each day relatively unscathed. We have learned to stay busy because if we slow down, we might actually feel our feelings, and let's be honest, that would be terrifying—and paralyzing. And who has time for that? We are tossing around toxic positivity just so that we can keep going. It is, after all, far too scary to *really see* the trouble we are in and the hardship we humans face individually and collectively. *Imposter syndrome* is rampant. With our self-esteem challenges, many of us feel undeserving of goodness even when it comes our way.

In all the busyness and demands of our lives, we have lost connection with one of our greatest resources, our bodies. Giving all the power to our thinking minds, we use our bodies to stash and hide things away, hoping that one day these things will just disappear. We might work out or go to yoga classes, but to actually feel our bodies can be frightening. This loss of connection with our bodies sits juxtaposed with our complete dependence on all things consumable, leading us to believe that what is tangible is somehow more real than anything happening inside ourselves. We have grown accustomed to believing that all of our scary feelings can be cured with something outside ourselves, something physical, something consumable. Our challenging relationship with food—and nourishment in general, is no doubt a by-product of this disconnection.

As a consequence, we have abandoned ourselves and lost connection with our intuition—that which originally made us powerful and unique beings. We know we have strayed far and many of us are ashamed of our bodies and thoughts—becoming victims of our own lives. We look in the mirror and no longer recognize who we have become. We live in fear that we do not belong— even to this world. Our hearts are broken, our grief is immense.

What is happening in our mind is simply a mirror for the trauma that is living in our nervous systems. *Trauma* is not always big and loud—wars, violence, natural disasters, shootings, car accidents, rape, and other horrors. Trauma can also be quiet and insidious. Unlike the saber-toothed tiger of times past, our modern-day predator has become, more commonly, an accumulation of the stress of our relationships, our jobs, our finances, our health, our families, our obligations, and our other day-to-day experiences that are overwhelming and not aligned with who we feel we are or want to be. These day-to-day exposures to stressful experiences—even though they may seem minor—add up. We are taking so much on each day just to manage our lives that we are already living on the upper end of what we can tolerate. Our nervous systems have reached maximum capacity.

I have come to understand trauma as a survival strategy that most humans will experience in their lifetimes. It is not only an emotional response; it is also *somatic* (soma, meaning body). It is a protective measure that happens in the body, signaling to us that there is a threat (real or perceived, it doesn't matter to our nervous system), and we must respond if we are to survive. Unlike psychology's historical reflections on trauma, it is not an event. Three people can experience a car accident, for example, and only one person might become traumatized. The difference among these three people is a matter of underlying risk and resiliency factors as well as timely access to resources. Trauma has become, well—normalized. However, what isn't normal about trauma is when trauma stays embedded in the body and psyche and continues to impact us for decades.

What is happening in our nervous systems is a mirror of the unhealed trauma stuck in our bodies and psyches. Unhealed trauma lives in our nervous systems and keeps us ramped up in a state of hypervigilance and in survival mode. This state is what makes us vulnerable to the stories we carry about ourselves and our lives, to the stories others carry about us, and even to cultural messaging. Unhealed trauma living in our nervous system dissolves our sense of safety, invades our boundaries, and creates vulnerability inside of us to whatever is happening in the environment. Unhealed trauma leaves us feeling separate.

As if all of this wasn't hard enough, unhealed trauma also inhibits our ability to play, imagine, and dream (3). This impact on our brain can make it difficult to appreciate music and art or to express creativity or make meaning from our life experiences because our ability to experience symbolism and to *think outside the box* has been pushed far outside of our reach. It is no wonder that many of us cannot even imagine our lives differently than the way we are living now. This impact leaves us like prey to the dominant paradigm.

It feels important to make it explicit here, while we are just getting started in our work together, that *you are not at the mercy of trauma.* Trauma can be transformed, which is why it is vital that you learn to identify it, have compassion for the ways your psyche and your life has accommodated its repercussions, and learn to work toward healing.

Trauma does not heal and go away on its own. In fact, the more we ignore it, the more likely it will come out sideways at the most inopportune times. Trauma needs tending. By tending to our trauma, we become more understanding, more compassionate toward ourselves and others, and more resilient to the ups and downs of our unpredictable human lives. Get in there and do the work and yet maintain a sense of trust that underneath your trauma responses lives a healthy, resilient being—a being who is ready to call out and reject the unhealthy and unsustainable aspects of the dominant culture. A being who is ripening perfectly for these beautiful and challenging times, who is longing for wholeness, and who won't settle for less. Can you trust that?

AN INVITATION:
Bridging the Inner and Outer Landscapes

Trauma responses take our awareness from the inside, from our own bodies and minds, and place it on the outside. The wisdom aspect of this, of course, is that we feel we need to track the perceived threat. The problem is that over time, and after the perceived threat has disappeared, we have been conditioned to track the environment and other people *more than we track ourselves*. This is dangerous territory to be in as it is a symptom of the severance from our body and its wisdom—a powerful resource. And yet this is all too common.

When we are too busy tracking the outer landscape, we are not paying attention to our vital cues in our inner landscape. This means our own intuition and our own body's needs are no longer top priority, leaving us even more vulnerable to traumatic experiences. Reversing this process is one way of supporting your body to come out of a traumatized state/sympathetic nervous system response and into a parasympathetic/resourced state. And breathing is an accessible resource that can take us there, bridging both worlds.

Breathing is a free, powerful resource that you have access to 24/7, and it not only keeps you alive, but when breathing properly you are less likely to become stuck in a trauma response. Improper breathing can actually exacerbate feelings of stress and anxiety because it unconsciously keeps you in a state of mild hyperventilation—leading to a perceived threat response. Many of us are used to living our lives in this state.

Learning to breathe properly and through especially difficult emotions and experiences can serve us in many ways, including lessening the long-term impact, lessening the intensity, and supporting our movement through and integration of the emotions and/or difficult experience. I will introduce you to one of my favorite breathing techniques that I use almost daily as a way to continue to repattern my nervous system for wellness and to counter any habituated trauma responses.

Plant Breathing

Plants and humans have been in a symbiotic relationship since the beginning of time. We need each other, in fact. At the most fundamental level, we humans need the continuous release of oxygen from plants so that we can breathe. And plants need our continuous exhale of carbon dioxide so that they can thrive. Without each other, we would die. We belong together.

Plant breathing not only supports us in connecting our inner and outer landscapes, but it also helps us regulate our nervous system, and it makes our interconnection with plants explicit. For this exercise, you can be indoors or outdoors (though I will always recommend getting outdoors if you are able), and all you need is a living plant to bring into your visual awareness (this includes trees, shrubs, herbs, flowers, and vines).

1. **Find a comfortable place to sit, stand, or lie down.** Ideally, find a place where you can see your chosen plant in your visual field without straining your head, neck, or eyes.

2. **Introduce yourself.** Say hello and introduce yourself in whatever way feels fitting for you at this moment.

3. **Imagine seeing the oxygen coming your way.** While looking at the plant, imagine you can see the oxygen it is releasing and imagine the plant is sending it directly to you.

4. **Inhale deeply.** Through your nose, bring this oxygen deep into your body. Feel it nourishing every cell it comes into contact with.

5. **Exhale completely.** Then as you exhale, purse your lips, blowing the carbon dioxide, sending it back to the plant.

6. **Match the length of your inhale with your exhale.** As much as you are able to without getting lightheaded, extend these exhales and inhales. See if you can match the length of your exhale with the length of your inhale.

7. **Send breath into your emotion.** Identify an emotion present in your body and/or mind. On your next inhale, imagine this breath moving oxygen from the plant through your body, and directly into the emotion you identified.

8. **Exhale your emotion back to the plant.** On your next exhale, purse your lips and blow some of your emotion along with the carbon dioxide back to the plant. Repeat this inhale and exhale for five minutes.

9. **Offer gratitude.** After five minutes, or when you feel complete, thank the plant in whatever way feels good to you. I, personally, like to place my hand over my heart and say thank you out loud so that the vibrations of my gratitude in my voice and in my heart can be carried to the plant.

Next time you are feeling stressed or are experiencing an intense emotion, try breathing with plants. Notice what changes for you; the quality of your thoughts, the sensations in your body, or even your outlook on the near future. I invite you to take breaks as you read the following pages and make time for plant breathing. Research on healing from traumatic responses shows that simply long, slow breathing for a few minutes each day can shift a nervous system that is in a sympathetic, fight-or-flight state into a parasympathetic, rest and digest state (4). Imagine the healing that would be possible in your nervous system if you could breathe mindfully with the plants around you each day or even several times each day.

CHAPTER TWO:

TRAUMA LIVING IN OUR NERVOUS SYSTEMS

IN WESTERN SOCIETY, we have normalized many trauma responses, chalking them up to personality or behavior. Trauma responses are symptoms of a *nervous system* that is stuck in an under-resourced state. Learning to recognize them in yourself and in others can support you in understanding how you, and your loved ones, process stress and/or trauma, develop compassion for these patterned responses, and begin the process of tending to them so they have the opportunity to heal. As Krishnamurti says, "It is no measure of health to be well adjusted to a profoundly sick society."

By nervous system, I am referring to the collective functioning of the brain, spinal cord, and nerves, whose sole job is to send and receive messages from inside and outside of the body. This constant feedback loop enables us to track the environment for changes and, most certainly, for threats. As mammals, when we feel threatened, our nervous systems are often patterned to respond in one of four ways: fight, flight, freeze, and fawn. These responses are not static. We can swing in and out of each of them (sometimes in a matter of an hour or over days, weeks, months, and years); however, we do typically have a default response that becomes patterned over time:

✦ **Fighting** leads to attempting to survive the experience by becoming aggressive.

✦ **Fleeing** leads to attempting to survive the experience by escaping.

✦ **Freezing** leads to attempting to survive the experience by shutting down (can also resemble psychological dissociation).

✦ **Fawning**, a newly understood strategy first described by author and therapist Pete Walker, MA, MFT, leads to attempting to survive by immediately moving into an appeasing state.

Sadly, fawning has become normalized in our society, which is why I want to focus on it here. Fawning can appear in a number of ways, including automatically agreeing with others, appeasing others, responding to others by saying what you know they want to hear, and writing off your own needs in an attempt to avoid conflict. Fawning can also look like staying in close relationships with others who have historically not been emotionally or physically safe. The wisdom aspect of this survival strategy is that if you keep what threatens you close, you can track it better than if it is farther away. Fawning frequently gets chalked up to personality rather than to a survival strategy. And getting stuck in an appeasing state is a sure sign of a trauma response.

Fawning is a response to a threat that is generated by the social engagement branch of the autonomic nervous system. Since estrogen is, among other things, a bonding hormone, when experiencing threat, it can make those who have more estrogen more likely to seek safety through human connection first before eliciting the responses of the other aspects of the nervous system, such as fighting, fleeing, or freezing. Therefore, fawning tends to occur more frequently for those who fall on the more feminine end of the masculine-feminine spectrum. However, fawning is a trauma response that can ultimately appear for anyone.

Often fawning behavior begins when we are young, and the trauma we are experiencing is happening with persons of trust. Because *neurons that fire together wire together* (thank you, Donald Hebb), we learn from a young age to link our experiences with what was happening in the environment at the time in an effort to anticipate danger. When we learn that conflict often precedes challenging emotions or experiences, we develop strategies to avoid it. Adopting appeasing behavior is an extremely common response.

Our society rewards fawning and because of this, we are at greater risk of getting stuck in this trauma response—often without our conscious awareness. How many times have you found yourself saying, "yes!" when every fiber of your being has wanted to shout, "hell no!" How many times have you overrode your inner voice in exchange for keeping the peace? How many times have you been encouraged to *be the bigger person* by not reacting to a personal violation? These might be fawning behaviors worthy of deeper examination.

Fawning trauma responses teach us to forego our own needs to stay in a real or perceived sense of safety. Though each time we write off one of our needs, whether it be for safety, to maintain a sense of connection, to feel loved, and so on, those needs don't simply disappear. As a survival strategy, once we realize we can't get our needs met, we learn to sever from them. In psychology, we call this *fragmentation,* and it explains why we frequently feel like we don't know what we need or we have conflicting feelings when a need arises (as in, I both need it and I have also learned to get by without it at the same time). Fragmentation is a form of dissociation and is what has led us to wind up in situations (relationships, careers, lifestyles, social or religious groups, even with personalities, etc.) that are not aligned with who we feel we truly are. Fragmentation is the opposite of full embodiment. We get ourselves into all kinds of misaligned situations when we are fragmented. Yet, those underlying needs can and will always reappear later, usually when it feels wildly inconvenient.

Many of us are also living our lives as though we are in a collective, trauma-freeze response. How else could we allow so much suffering of our fellow humans and animals, so much degradation to our planet, while at the same time, we are stopping for our regular lattes and going about our days? There is a disconnect between what we know in our bones and the way we are living our lives. In our frozen state, we have exchanged our need for real safety, community, deep nourishment, belonging, and authentic self-expression for a perceived sense of safety and superficial, temporary nourishment. On the surface, we have become complacent, and this is what makes us humans so dangerous right now—to ourselves, to each other, and to the Earth. Yet, if we can pause long enough to look underneath all the challenging behaviors, we will find significant unhealed trauma embedded in the bodies of our people. Our behaviors, however confusing, reveal our longing to get our needs met and our desire for healing.

While it may feel more familiar—and temporarily more comfortable—to numb out, busy yourself, or run away from your pain, if you want to deepen your relationship with yourself and make space for healing, you must learn to challenge these habits. You must learn to turn your awareness inward and attune to your own needs rather than outward, habitually attuning to the needs of others and to the *shoulds* of society. It is important, especially now, while the stakes are so high, to give yourself the space (and resources needed) to feel your emotions.

These losses are not only exterior losses, but they are also losses of parts of ourselves. Each time we look at a landscape as it is scraped, pummeled, drilled, and otherwise altered, our bodies and psyches are also scraped, pummeled, drilled, and altered. Though you have your vices and your perceived buffers, you can't help but to feel repercussions from the damage done to the Earth because you are, after all, not separate from her.

Emotion can be scary. For some to open Pandora's box of emotion could mean a total life takeover. Permission to feel may leave you exposed, raw, vulnerable, as though you are drowning, unable to ground or feel hopeful once again. I know I have found myself in this territory many times before. This is in part because we have not been taught to feel our emotions. We are instead taught to *pick ourselves up by our bootstraps* and keep going at all costs. However, like a dam in a river, emotion can stagnate. Learning to let the water out slowly in a nurturing way is wildly supportive to the healing process.

The capacity to experience the full spectrum of human emotion is needed if you are to tend to the root of your traumas, and this may mean welcoming emotions from long, long ago. If you are concerned about opening up a deep well of emotion and being unable to close it and carry on with your day afterward, I want to invite you to *titrate* your emotions. *Titration* is used to describe our ability to take the perfect-sized bite of what you are able to process at any given moment, not too big and not too small. This practice is helpful when working with intense emotions and/or experiences so that you are able to stay within your unique bandwidth, known as the *window of tolerance*.

Window of Tolerance

One incredibly helpful tool used in psychology to deepen our understanding of this concept of having a personal bandwidth is called the window of tolerance. Coined by Daniel Siegel, MD, the window of tolerance is a term used to describe our nervous system's capacity for stress (1). The window of tolerance is a unique window that each one of us has for our life experiences and can support us in understanding when and why you may feel overwhelmed or even traumatized by an experience, as well as when you feel appropriately challenged.

Stress is not always a negative experience. Think of it in terms of degrees of pressure. In fact, the perfect amount of pressure can create motivation and inspiration, propelling your life forward to reach your personal and professional goals. Too little pressure and you can feel unambitious, bored, and uninspired. The goal—and what I hope to present in the work that we are doing together—is to stay within your window of tolerance and yet to appropriately challenge you with the various strategic and thoughtful invitations presented throughout this book. Appropriate challenges will enable you to stretch and grow your emotional capacity, leaving you less vulnerable and more resilient against traumatic experiences.

In a perfect world, you want a fairly wide window of tolerance. When you are operating within a wide window of tolerance, you are able to cope with life's experiences reasonably well. You meet challenges with energy and creativity; you feel alert but not anxious, calm but not wiped out. This is not a state of utopia, but rather a place where you are resilient, you feel connected, flexible, where you can ride the waves of life's ups and downs, emotion, sensation, and can feel a sense of buoyancy in your nervous system. In this state, you trust you have the capacity to come back home to yourself even after extremely challenging experiences.

When you are operating within a narrow window of tolerance, you will feel less resilient, more separate and rigid, and more vulnerable to stress. Unexpected hardship and chronic exposure to stress without timely access to resources can more easily take you outside of your window of tolerance (time is in and of itself a resource, after all). When you are outside of your window of tolerance and do not have the resources to move back into your window within an appropriate amount of time, the chances of experiencing trauma and getting stuck in a trauma response become quite high.

The difference between a wide and narrow window of tolerance is *experience* combined with *resources*. Your window of tolerance expands only at the same rate that you can have experiences that are matched with access to resources. Trauma happens when you have an experience that was not met with the appropriate or timely resources, leaving your psyche and nervous system operating outside of your window of tolerance. This is why children are so vulnerable to trauma: they have not yet built a database of life experiences, and since children resource themselves mostly through contact with their caregivers, they are dependent on a healthy, present adult to be available to support them in quickly moving back inside their window of tolerance. More on this in part two.

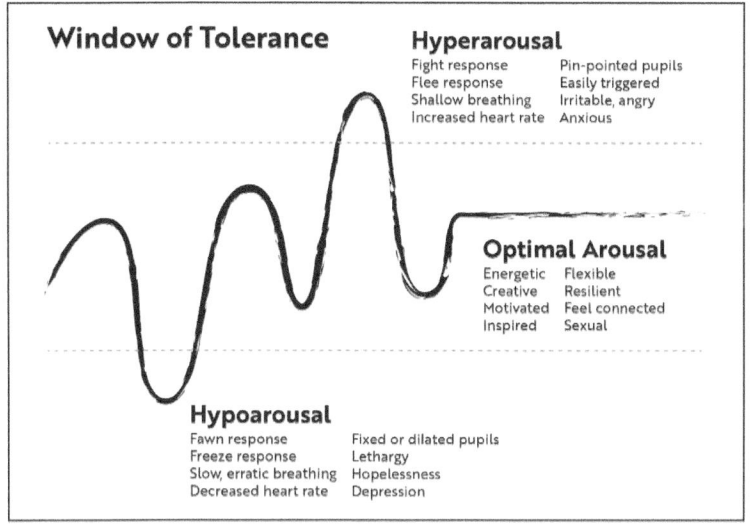

Responses to operating outside of your window of tolerance can look vastly different. As you can see in the scale, on one end, you have symptoms of hyperarousal, and on the other end, hypoarousal. Hyperarousal corresponds with urges to fight or flee and is often accompanied by shallow breathing, increased heart rate, pin-pointed pupils, and feeling easily triggered and anxious. When you are in a state of hyperarousal, you are likely to feel a surge of stress hormones, mostly adrenaline and cortisol.

On the other end of the window of tolerance, you have the symptoms of hypoarousal. This state corresponds with the fawn or freeze response in the nervous system and is often accompanied by slow, erratic breathing, decreased heart rate, dilated or fixed pupils, lethargy, hopelessness, and depression. (Depression is often the result of a prolonged freeze response in the nervous system.) When you are in a state of hypoarousal, you are likely to feel suddenly or chronically exhausted as you've had an unexpected dip or prolonged lack of stress hormones. Of note, we do need some access to stress hormones to be healthy. Balanced stress hormones provide an appropriate amount of energy: not too much and not too little, with energy that waxes and wanes throughout each day.

The window of tolerance is not a fixed state, rather it is fluid. Some days you may wake up with a wider window and other days it may feel more narrow. The difference here has to do with resources. If you slept well (an excellent resource), woke up in the morning and ate nourishing food (another great resource), and had a moment to yourself before engaging in the active part of your day (yet another wonderful resource), you may find yourself with a wider bandwidth. If however, you slept horribly, shoved a few bites of leftover takeout in your mouth, hopped into your car only to hit traffic and run late for work, and then found yourself soon afterward sitting at the desk of a job you really don't jive with, your bandwidth is likely going to be quite small.

Taking note of where your personal bandwidth may be on any given day can make the difference between welcoming an appropriate challenge or re-traumatizing yourself. This is why I wanted to introduce you to the window of tolerance now. I will be inviting you again and again into practices throughout this book that will require some engagement with material that you may discover brings up intense emotion and/or sensation. While I wish we could sit side by side on the Earth engaging in these practices together (opportunities to do this work with me can be found in the resource section at the end of this book), since we are not, I won't be able to support you directly in tracking your nervous system's arousal as you navigate this material. Therefore, I ask that you track your level of arousal, titrate your emotion, and stay within your window of tolerance during these invitations.

Staying within your window of tolerance doesn't mean you are denying the full depth of your experience. It simply means that you will be allowing your nervous system to assess, chew, swallow, and rest after each bite before taking another. For example, instead of opening up to the grief of the immense suffering of the animals on our planet, titrate your grief by working with the grief you have for your own pet or a wild animal being who you feel kinship with first. Without this capacity to gauge your personal window of tolerance as you explore the terrain I am introducing, you run the risk of winding up outside of it. So please do take the best care of yourself by pausing and checking in frequently and looking for any of the above-mentioned clues that you may be heading outside of your window.

Risk and Resiliency Factors

There are certain identifiable risk and resiliency factors that come into play in early life that can predispose you to a narrow window of tolerance well into adulthood. These factors influence your level of vulnerability to experiencing trauma and to your success or challenge in navigating and healing from trauma responses. As you will notice in the list of risk factors, the overarching theme is the lack of internal and external resources.

Risk Factors

1. Family environment that is NOT supportive or nurturing

2. Family relationships that are NOT dependable or stable

3. Lack of appropriate affection from parents or caregivers

4. Financial instability

5. Lack of academic achievement, reduced cognitive exposure or capacity

6. Parents/caregivers who are not healthy, mentally and/or physically

7. Prior experience of trauma or exposure to extremely stressful events*

8. Prenatal and perinatal trauma experience such as hypoxia

9. Limited coping mechanisms

*This includes the impact of racism, sexism, ageism, ableism, classism, fatism, homophobia, transphobia, xenophobia, religious prejudice, and other forms of oppression experienced either personally, ancestrally, or collectively.

Opposite risk factors, each of us individually and collectively have resiliency factors. When it comes to resiliency, the overarching theme is the availability of internal and external resources.

Resiliency Factors

1. Opportunities to discuss, debrief, or otherwise engage in healing activities

2. Secure and nurturing family and community

3. Appropriate amounts of risk and boundaries as a child

4. Access to education

5. Social competence and meaningful relationships

6. Physical health

7. Financial stability

8. Personal goals and aspirations, a sense of purpose

9. A sense of humor, empathy, and, in general, a positive outlook on life

10. Belief in something larger than oneself

When you have a high amount of risk factors and a low amount of resiliency factors, simply put—you are at a greater risk for experiencing trauma and becoming stuck in a trauma response after exposure to extreme stress. When you have a low amount of risk factors and a high amount of resiliency factors, the chances of experiencing trauma or getting stuck in a trauma response after exposure to extreme stress are much more slim.

A large part of your healing journey must include moving from the high-risk category over to the high-resiliency category and this movement is 100 percent dependent on the building of resources, both internal and external. While it can be natural to assume that this movement happens rapidly with access to financial resources, research actually shows us something different. In fact, children raised in an *affluent* household it turns out, tend to develop less emotional resiliency than children who are raised without access to financial resources (2). While money can give us access to some resiliency factors, it can actually inhibit access to others. Therefore, developing resiliency must include building a variety of internal and external resources.

Looking at this list of risk and resiliency factors, where do you see yourself falling? Take note. This is important information for you to know about yourself and to hold with tenderness and care.

To empower you with tools and resources needed during our work together, I want to invite you to continue practicing titration as needed during your reading of the following material. Because I really want you to experience the healthy repatterning of your nervous system, I want to give you every opportunity to use the material we are exploring—not later once you have finished reading this material but now, while we are in it together. Therefore, I recommend practicing titrating after every chapter. And when you find you are in a state of hyper- or hypoarousal, are no longer absorbing the material, or your mind is wandering far, take a break. How are you doing right now, by the way? Do you need a minute before moving on to the invitation to practice? Can you feel your body? Listen.

AN INVITATION:
Building Shame Tolerance

One human-centric emotion that many of us have lost our ability to tolerate is that of shame. In fact, I believe that shame sits at the center of so many acts of violence, including many of the recent mass shootings in the US. How many of these shooters have been bullied, recluses, or otherwise not following the status quo? Shame is a purely negative motivator and our intolerance of it can drive us to do nearly *anything* to get away from its experience. Yet most of us carry the pain of shame around in our psyches and bodies. I believe it is also one factor underlying perfectionism and overachievement, as well as depression, lack of motivation, fatigue, and suicide. Why do you think most people, even the most incredible and empowered people in the world, say they would rather die than speak publicly?

Though they are frequently paired together in conversations, shame and *guilt* are not the same thing. Instead of, "I did something bad," which is the messaging behind the emotion of guilt, shame tells us, "I *am* bad." This messaging creates wildly different nervous system patterning because instead of having an experience of *doing something bad,* shame tells us *we are the bad thing.* This patterning can begin in infancy when there is chronic misattunement from the primary caregiver. In this situation, it becomes safer for a baby to think, *I am bad* than to think that her caregiver is bad. More on this in part two.

It is important to note that the experience of shame is a survival strategy. If you are in a shameful place, you will be less likely to take risks, make changes, and speak up for yourself or for others. In this way, shame is keeping you in a state of perceived safety. However, it is also limiting you, your expression, and life choices because then you are always at its mercy. As shame is part of the human condition, working with building more tolerance for it is a strategy that will help you integrate your life experiences and create more resilience in combating existing narratives about yourself and the world.

Because shame is such a powerful motivator in human behavior, it naturally arouses the sympathetic branch of the nervous system, providing you with sensations that most of us are all too familiar with racing heart, sweaty palms, trembling, jumbled thoughts, and the desire to fight, flee, freeze, or fawn. Therefore, part of learning to tolerate shame—instead of running from it, is learning to work with the sensations that arise in your body as the result of a shameful experience. Just like pain, we are patterned to want to avoid shame and do everything we can to make it go away, even if it means acting out of character. Learning your personal physiological response to shame can help you deconstruct it into smaller, more easily metabolized bites. When this happens, shame will no longer be a driving force in your nervous system and will, in fact, bring greater connection between you, your body, and your world.

This invitation will support you in building more shame tolerance, an essential first step on any healing journey. I developed this exercise inspired by the *Good Parent Messages, the* work of Dr. Jack Rosenberg from Integrative Body Psychotherapy.

1. **Locate a story of shame.** When you are feeling resourced and in a safe place in your body and psyche, consider an experience where you felt ashamed of something. Ideally, choose an experience that is in the past and brings up no more charge in your body than a level five out of ten. Remember to stay within your window of tolerance. Travel back to that moment, reliving it in your mind. What exactly happened? Bring as many details to the forefront as you are able to.

2. **Find the underlying message.** Shame often carries messages with it, which we then download and repeat to ourselves throughout our lifetimes. Is there a message that accompanies your story? What did

your psyche and nervous system download from this experience? I will provide some examples, and I encourage you to take some time here and find the exact message (or several) that feeds into your experience of shame. You will recognize the message that hits close to home when there is a shift in your level of arousal:

a. I am a bad person.
b. I am not worthy of love.
c. I am not trustworthy.
d. No one has my back.
e. I deserved this.
f. There is something wrong with me.

3. **Notice the sensations that accompany this story of shame.** Once you have located the message, drop the story that brought you to it and simply say the accompanying message out loud to yourself several times in a row. Feel your body and its sensations as you do this. Remember to titrate if the sensations feel too intense and/or are taking you outside of your window of tolerance. What is happening in your body? Specifically, how is your breathing? Is it deep or shallow? Is your heart rate fast or slow, or erratic? And what is your body temperature? Do you feel hot? Cold? Hot in your core with cold hands and feet? Are your cheeks flushed? Is there a sensation somewhere in your body where energy feels stuck? In your throat? Or in your abdomen? Deconstruct these sensations into the smallest parts possible. Instead of simply, *I feel cold*, where do you feel cold? How cold? Freezing, or? Take detailed note of the sensations you are feeling in your body. These are the sensations that are alerting you of this potential threat your body knows as *shame*.

4. **Take regulating breaths.** Place one hand on your body where you feel the shame sensation and begin taking long, slow breaths. Imagine yourself inhaling and bringing your breath right into the location of the shame sensation and then exhaling, sending some of the sensation back into the Earth. Do any of the sensations change when you do this? Keep breathing like this until you feel a shift or for at least five minutes.

5. **Find the antidote message.** Next, I want you to find the antidote message(s) to the message(s) you discovered earlier. The only rule is that it has to start with "I." As you try on the examples provided below, track which one has the greatest neutralizing effect on the level of arousal in your nervous system. I recommend saying each of the messages out loud. You will notice when you hear the most resonant message because you will feel as though someone just poured warm honey on an old wound when you hear it spoken. Once you've found it, say this message out loud to yourself several times.

   a. I am a good person.
   b. I am lovable.
   c. I trust you.
   d. I am here for you.
   e. I deserve goodness.
   f. I am perfect as I am.

6. **Savor the goodness.** Since part of the negative impact of traumatic experience involves becoming hypervigilant and learning to track the environment only for threats, we can often miss good things when they are happening. Therefore, learning to savor goodness is important. Give yourself permission to stay in this state, repeating your antidote message for as long as you are able. Trust its healing power.

Shame *can* be healed. The next time you feel shame sensations welling up in your body, consider taking these steps to unpack and deconstruct the messaging underneath. As you do this over and over again, you will gain more familiarity with your felt sense of shame and, as a result, widen your window of tolerance.

A client of mine named Callie, who had recently accepted a promotion into a leadership position at her job, reached out to me struggling with intense shame. "The shame," she said, "is making me sick. My stomach constantly feels like a ball of clay sitting heavy in my abdomen." She said she had struggled with it for most of her life but that it was now rearing its head whenever she was asked to present something to her coworkers, which was becoming more frequent in this new role. She would start worrying days before, losing hours of sleep and skipping meals. Then when the day came, her face would flush red, her jaw would tremble, and she would sweat through whatever shirt she was wearing—the smelly, stress kind of sweat. Despite many of her presentations going fairly well, afterward, she would berate herself over what she said and how she said it, ruminating for days. This only created more shame in her system.

When we started working together, she mentioned being kind of a quiet, introverted child, very much into making art and spending time in nature. She chalked her fear of public speaking up to it not being in her nature. However, as I got to know more of her history and, specifically, more about her mother, I was wondering if the shame Callie was experiencing wasn't in fact her mother's own shame that she had now internalized.

When we internalize something, we are often unconsciously assimilating an attitude, belief, or behavior that is outside of ourselves and making it our own. When Callie was a child, her mother would openly criticize her for numerous things, including the outfits she chose, the books she was reading, and even each time she was trying to learn a new skill like playing an instrument or baking.

I am never surprised to learn that when people in our lives treat us this way, it often reflects only a fraction of the criticism they give themselves. However, without knowing that, Callie took on her mom's criticism and developed the belief that she was not worthy of love. With this core belief running rampant in her psyche and setting the foundation of her nervous system patterning, experiences like presenting to her coworkers became another avenue for which she would be reminded that she was not worthy of love.

Mine and Callie's work together became focused on unpacking some of this internalized shame, deconstructing her felt bodily sensations of shame as well as working with the "I am lovable" messaging. She learned to breathe directly into the dense, ball-of-clay sensation in her belly, to give it more space, and to eventually feel it grow smaller and smaller until it was undetectable. She learned to place her hands on her cheeks and her jaw, where she would feel a tremendous amount of sensation during a shame experience, and tell herself how lovable she was even when she was afraid. As she did this powerful healing work over several months, she was slowly able to separate her mom's shame from her own and build more shame tolerance in her body, psyche, and nervous system, thereby widening her window of tolerance.

AN INVITATION:
Gathering Your Personal Resources

To continue our work together in widening your window of tolerance, I want to support you in the gathering of your personal *resources*. Remember, growing a wide window of tolerance includes having life experiences that are matched by your access to personal resources. By "resources" I am referring to the physical, emotional, and spiritual support each one of us draws upon to help us in times of need. Your resources could be special connections with friends, family members, therapists, other practitioners, and even pets. They could also be nourishing practices such as meditation, breathing techniques, exercising, journaling, taking walks in nature, taking baths, or connecting with a spiritual or religious practice or prayer. Or they could be physical items such as pictures of a loved one or spiritual teacher, stones, jewelry, a piece of fabric, incense, feathers, etc.

Remembering that you belong to the Earth can become a primary resource for you. It's easy to take this relationship for granted because Earth is *always there*. When you wake, you just know that she will be under your feet. Not to mention, we humans have evolved so perfectly for this planet from our feet that enable us to traverse her surface, to our senses that enable us to witness and feel her aliveness, to our vulnerability to her gravitational pull, to our lungs that so perfectly exchange oxygen and carbon dioxide with the plants. We are not separate from her; we were made of and for her.

Each one of us has our own unique pool of resources that we draw from every day. It's important that you find out what personal resources you are already drawing from so that you can strengthen your connection with them and also see where you might have some gaps. As you have gathered, the more resources you have access to, the less vulnerable you are to chronic stress and trauma.

How do you know what your personal resources are? I invite you to begin a process of looking at and naming your resources through a practice that I have found most helpful. I call it a *process* because gathering and naming resources is not static; it is dynamic, and you always have the opportunity to grow your pool of them. This activity will support you in building a relationship with some of your natural and existing resources. I want you to be most familiar with these as these will keep you grounded through our work together and also in your life outside of these pages. It's always a good idea to have this list handy so that you can grab it in times of need, especially during times of high stress when you are more vulnerable to experiencing trauma.

1. **Pull out three sheets of blank or lined paper and a pencil or pen, whatever your pleasure.** I want you to write, at the top of each piece of paper, one sentence about a big life event that you survived. This could be something that you would consider one of your life's greatest challenges. For this exercise, these must be challenges that you have overcome—not challenges you are currently facing. Here are some examples:

   + The birth of my child.
   + The death of my loved one.
   + A trauma such as a car accident or natural disaster.
   + A separation or divorce.
   + Abuse by a person of trust.
   + The miscarriage of my child.

2. **Working on one life challenge/one sheet of paper at a time, list the tools you used to overcome this challenge.** Consider these questions: How did you survive? What got you through it? What tools did you

43

have? Which people were around you? Who did you call on (living or not)? What practices got you by? These tools could be friends, family, memories (imagined or real), places, physical items, foods, herbs, and/or treatments such as acupuncture or bodywork. They could even be a mythical or archetypal figure; you get to name it because it was your process.

Some tools that you may have used to survive might not be resources that you feel particularly proud of, and that's okay. For example, if you were to freeze instead of fight, distract yourself with substances like drugs or alcohol, or if you were to get on anti-depressants to survive the consequences of the experience, you may hold some shame about these reactions. However, freezing instead of fighting, fleeing, or fawning could have allowed you to survive the experience if you were outnumbered or outpowered. Drugs and alcohol may have buffered your psyche from this horrible experiences for a period of time. And antidepressants may have done the same. Please know that the point of this exercise is not to shame yourself or judge your resources. Each resource, even the ones that you aren't proud of, have to be seen in their wisdom at the time they were called upon.

Write all of your resources down on the piece of paper for each major life event. Here's an example:

When I was fifteen, I was attacked by a neighbor and friend of the family. He shoved me into a closet and sexually assaulted me. (This is where you write briefly about the event you survived)

I survived because... (This is where you write about how you survived, the tools, people, and practices you engaged in)

+ *I had the instinct to freeze*
+ *I dissociated from my body*
+ *I got into therapy three years later*
+ *I shared my experience with my aunt, who is a healthy, loving family member*
+ *I went on antidepressants for five years*
+ *I found a group of other women who had similar experiences and was able to give and receive support*
+ *I talked with my best friend about it*
+ *I became hypervigilant about the older men in my life*
+ *I started drinking chamomile tea before bed to help with nightmares*

3. **Once you've filled out your three sheets of paper, I invite you to lay them out on a table so you can see them all at once and notice the repetitive phrases or words.** What are the top ten or fifteen words that were repeated with each challenge that you overcame in your life?

4. **On a separate sheet of paper, gather those words onto one list.** Here, you have your most prized possessions: your personal resource list. Here is a list of resources some of my students have shared:

+ Deep breathing
+ Visiting the ocean, large rivers, mountains, vast open spaces
+ A partner or lover
+ Spending time with four-legged beings
+ Memories of a healthy ancestor
+ Sitting at the base of large, old trees
+ Herbal tea (especially adaptogenic herbs)
+ A long night's sleep
+ Hot baths, especially hot springs in nature
+ Close friendships

✦ Rose quartz in my pocket

✦ Seeing images of our beautiful planet Earth

✦ Looking at your family tree (reminding you that you've come from somewhere)

✦ Acupressure on stabilizing places in your body

✦ Smelling essential oils

✦ Your therapist/healer

✦ Acupuncture treatments

✦ Walking slowly enough to feel your feet on the Earth

5. **For each item on your list that is tangible, bring that item to your visual field as you journey onward through these next pages.** You will want those items to be visible to you regularly while we dive deeper in together so that you remember them and utilize them. You could even gather them all together and create a *resource altar* in your home that you visit each day and are reminded of all that supports you on your healing journey.

6. **For each item on your list that is intangible or that you are unable to gather physically, I want you to go out into the natural world and find an object that represents it.** This could be a rock, a fallen branch, a tree or shrub, a mound of dirt, a leaf, a feather, you name it. Whatever you are called to identify will be the most perfect representation of that resource. Start with one thing at a time.

As you go down your list of intangible items, ask yourself: *how does this object represent my resource?* And speak out loud if you can about the qualities or characteristics of the natural object.

Abby, a client of mine, considers the ocean as one of her major resources. The last time she visited the ocean, she found a small, smooth seashell and brought it home with her to the mountains. She placed it next to her bed so that each time she woke up, she was reminded of the ocean and the calmness and security it brings her. During times of challenge, she would carry the seashell around with her in her pockets, feeling comforted by its smoothness between her fingers and reminded of the positive impact the ocean has on her nervous system.

May your list of resources continue to grow and grow throughout your life. If you are able to, consider carrying some of these tangible and accessible objects around with you in your pocket. Write and paste your list to your desk, and on the dashboard of your car. Look at it daily to build a stronger and stronger relationship with each person or practice that already supports and nourishes you. This is part of the healing wisdom already located in your inner landscape. You will need access to these as we journey onward into our personal, ancestral, and collective traumas in part two. Remember, your greatest resources will not be something that you need to go out and purchase, they are already available to you: the Earth, her beings, your body, and the people and practices that nourish you.

CHAPTER THREE:

OUR HUNTER-GATHERER SENSORY SYSTEMS

NOW THAT YOU UNDERSTAND more about how the human nervous system operates under threat, let's take a look at how our sensory system has evolved so that we can understand more of the impact unhealed trauma might have on us.

We humans are descendants of hunter-gatherer tribes that spanned more than 90 percent of human history. This means, for nearly two million years our sensory system has been built and honed as hunters and gatherers. For hunters, their primary roles often had to do with seeking out, stalking, hunting, and killing prey, and returning to the community with food in the form of bones, fur, skin, and meat. When our ancestors were hunting, their awareness needed to be placed solely on one thing: the prey. To track prey with a highly developed sensory system—they would use mostly their eyes and ears. As hunters, they developed and strengthened these senses to have a single-pointed focus so when they released their weapon, they would land exactly where they needed it to be. Many of us in the modern world primarily only use this part of our sensory system. We walk around with our agendas and our *hard, staring eyes,* eyes that have a single point of focus.

Gatherers, on the other hand, had to develop different skills. They would leave the tribe to go gather fruits, seeds, nuts, and vegetables from the land. Often they went in small groups and frequently brought their children with them and either carried them on their backs or made sure they played near them while they worked to gather food for the community. They would use their eyes, ears, sense of smell, sense of taste, and their felt sense to locate the best places to forage. Then, gently picking berries or digging up tubers, they would be simultaneously tracking for threats in their environment.

Therefore to ensure our safety, gatherer nervous systems learned to utilize many of their senses at once to track a larger, wider field of awareness and especially changes—however subtle, in that field of awareness. Even our skin and hair gave us valuable sensory feedback. What we now call "goosebumps" or "chicken skin" is the remnant of human evolution when we had hair that would stand on end when we felt a shift in the environment that felt potentially threatening. It is a part of our intuitive sensory feedback system. We can see this in dogs and other mammals who still have significant hair on their bodies. This capacity to multitask by using all of our sensory input: auditory, visual, olfactory, tasting, and feeling senses, became what we call *our intuition*.

Intuition is the combination of information gathered through our sensory system (sight, sound, smell, taste, and feeling), filtered through our past experiences. By *feeling*, I am referring to an accumulation of information gathered from our four senses combined with input from our digestive system and heart. Past experiences create a database of information that we have gathered and stored deep in our psyches and nervous systems. Our intuition is called upon when we are having an experience that reminds us of something from the past, indicating some kind of pattern has been recognized. Your psyche then assigns a meaning to this familiar pattern.

For example, the first time I heard a rustle in the bushes outside the front of my house, I explored it. I began to part the limbs of the bushes to see if I could see what was making that noise. Snake? Rabbit? Bird? Quickly I realized that a rabbit had made a home there. So now, when I hear that particular rustle, combined with my past experience of seeing the rabbit, I no longer need to look under the bush when I hear noises underneath; I can intuit that the rabbit is there. I have combined my sensory system with my past experiences and utilized my intuition.

As we filter through past experiences, we make meaning out of them. This feeling led to _____. This sound led to _____. It's a beautiful thing really because it enables us to collect information using the amazing instruments of our bodies as well as our unique past experiences. This ability to use our bodies as an instrument and our memory as a guidepost is incredible and is what has enabled us to survive for millions of years. We can use our intuition not only to stay safe but also use it to gather an immense amount of information about the world around us, including what is happening in our bodies, in our families, and in our world. A strong, clear, trustworthy intuition is like being able to see in the dark—it enables you to cut through distraction and know exactly what is going on. Intuition is not the same as being psychic—which is often linked with our cognition. Intuition, on the other hand, is 100 percent dependent on tracking feedback from our sensory system.

Of course, there is a shadow side to intuition when it has been impacted by trauma. If we have been busy gathering and storing data from a heightened, traumatized state, our sensory information may not be very trustworthy. This can lead us into the territory of *projection*. Projection is the (often) unconscious overlaying of old stories onto our current experiences and while they can be a natural response to trauma and created as a form of protection, they are not a reliable basis for intuition.

For example, if I have unhealed trauma after a horrible dog bite, I might think that I have intuited (i.e., projected) that most dogs will bite me if given the opportunity. And I might actually be right every once in a great while, which could reinforce this story. (In fact, the incongruent and fearful vibrations I carry in my traumatized nervous system might even cause a dog to bite me—especially if that dog has unhealed trauma with humans). There is nothing wrong with living at the mercy of our projections at certain moments on our healing journey; however, to stay stuck behind the stories they will inevitably create, we become anxious and more likely to misjudge the opportunities in our lives, seeing restrictions and challenges where there are none. The more we do our healing work, the more reliable and trustworthy our intuition becomes.

Intuition is an incredibly powerful aspect of our human sensory system. It is the ability to know something without analysis, reasoning, or deliberation—to know with our bodies. This requires an acute awareness of our internal signals, a capacity known as *interoception*. Interoceptive awareness is the ability to track internal body sensations. Tracking is something all mammals do. Tracking is a skill that happens both internally and externally, giving us important information about what is happening inside ourselves and in the environment. Recognizing our biological needs, such as the need to eat or to eliminate, happens because of our interoceptive awareness. As a survival strategy after experiencing trauma, we prioritize tracking the external environment over our internal environment. How many times have you missed or overridden a biological need in your busyness or overwhelm?

When trauma happens, there is frequently a part of us that says, "Hey, wait a minute! How did I let this happen?" As though you had control, as though you could have/should have seen it coming. More often than not, we blame ourselves—either consciously or unconsciously for "allowing" the bad thing to happen. This causes us to abandon our intuition.

Abandonment of our intuition is an abandonment of our body and its powerful ability to gather information through using its highly complex sensory system. When trauma happens and our relationship to our sensory system is severed, that's when we are in real trouble. We lose our ability to read (and trust) the world around us, and this leads to all kinds of challenges, including not knowing what is good for us and/or letting others tell us what is good for us. *How do we trust ourselves when such a large part of our sensory system has been taken offline?* Moving forward, we learn not to listen to the signs and signals: *they didn't protect us that time, so why would we expect them to protect us now?*

Tracking supports our personal sense of safety. However, when we can learn to track our environment with equal or greater attention to the tracking of our inner landscape, we open up a superpower. Not only does our interpretation of the world around us become more accurate, we can actually begin to *trust what we are sensing* and follow through with the responses and actions that feel most aligned. Strengthening our interoceptive awareness restores our connection with our own bodies as the powerful instruments that they are.

Think of it like this: if your intuition was intact, you would more easily repair your childhood wounds, you would know in your bones, the burdens that are personal versus the burdens that are ancestral or collective. You would know your personal value system and feel it when it is being manipulated by others or by cultural messaging. Ultimately, you would know when you are living out of alignment with yourself and be able to more quickly call yourself back home. Your intuition, after all, gifts you with a sense of empowerment as you walk through and interact with the world.

Disoriented to Health

We are influenced every day by the culture we live in, the good stuff and also the not-so-good stuff. It's as though without our consent, we are told who to be, how to perform, what to look like, how to behave, and worse, what to value from the dominant culture. This happens much more intensely for those who have untended trauma living in their nervous systems. This is because trauma responses that become stuck in our nervous systems disrupt our ability to resonate with that which is healthy. In psychology, we call this having a *disorientation to health*.

When trauma has left you disoriented to health, you can find it difficult to trust yourself and your own instincts and to decipher which decisions are arising from your authentic voice and which ones are internalized from outside sources. In our disorientation, our *inner compass*—the part of us guided by our intuition, can be calibrated to another Universe entirely—leading us into a life that is misaligned with who we truly are, what we genuinely need, and what we came here to do.

However, underneath all the challenges you have had in your life and underneath all the residue they left behind, trust that you have a completely intact, whole powerful sensory system living inside of you. In fact, I would say that *because of these challenging experiences,* you have the opportunity to have an even stronger capacity to intuit than those who have not (more on this later). This is because of the tracking power of your sensory system that becomes heightened after a traumatic experience. However, you have also learned through others and through repeated difficult experiences to bulldoze over your own instincts as a way to get by. But trust that they are still underneath these habituated responses giving you valuable information; you just have to relearn how to use them and then regain your sense of trust in them.

So, how do you learn to intuit confidently, given that you may have a history of ignoring or bypassing your own intuition? How do you reopen this ancient and vital part of your hunter-gatherer sensory system and let its wisdom permeate your life and restore a sense of safety inside yourself? How do you learn to trust your sensory system feedback once again? You must learn to recalibrate your inner compass.

AN INVITATION:
Recalibrating Your Inner Compass

As humans, we all *want* to resonate with what is healthy—physically, mentally, spiritually, and emotionally. We all want to feel safe and free at home inside ourselves. But sometimes, the information we are getting from our nervous system's feedback loop is confusing because health can become a foreign concept when you have unhealed trauma living in your nervous system. So you must first learn to reestablish a direct connection with yourself, with your own inner compass. In trauma work, we call this *orienting*. Animals in the wild are constantly orienting, and we humans are no different. There are two types of orienting: defensive orienting and exploratory orienting.

Defensive orienting is when we are using our powerful sensory system to survey the environment for threats. Defensive orienting happens when we sense a sudden change in the environment, whether it is an unfamiliar sound or we think we saw something and we immediately orient our senses to the perceived threat. An example is when I am hiking in the desert and hear the sound of a rattle, I pause immediately and look around me to see if there is in fact a rattlesnake. This is a healthy, balanced aspect of defensive orienting.

A deer, for example, might be busy eating grass but then hear a noise and suddenly pop its head and ears straight up to orient to the potential threat. This is also a healthy response. The deer is orienting to the sound, sight, and feeling of a shift in the environment to assess threats.

An imbalanced version of defensive orienting is most prevalent in us humans today. This happens when you are in a place that is relatively safe and yet you can't stop looking around, listening, and trying to locate threats in the environment. This would be like if I am hiking and can't enjoy myself because

I am too busy looking for rattlesnakes even though I haven't heard or seen one all season. Unhealed trauma responses cause us to become hypervigilant in a similar way, tracking the environment for threats to maintain a perceived sense of safety. Processing the environment in this way can become habitual and is all too common today—and not just in the wild—in our everyday lives.

Exploratory orienting, on the other hand, happens only when we feel safe and is a wonderful first step to learning to reorient our inner compass. It is a pleasurable form of orienting, like watching the sunset. When children feel safe, we see them do this all the time. They will look around their environment and pick up on things that might not be so ordinary to see, usually bringing them delight and a desire to share their observations. This is a wonderful sign of health.

In adults, exploratory orienting requires a feeling of safety, relaxation in the nervous system, slowness, and connection between what is happening inside with what is happening outside of ourselves. This is the ultimate experience of feeling at home inside ourselves. Exploratory orienting can look like a number of different experiences, such as the ability to look around the environment and notice things like a unique plant or tree or to go for a walk or some kind of adventure without a particular agenda. It is a type of casual play opportunity that emerges only when we are feeling at home inside ourselves. Playfulness, after all, is one of the first things to disappear after we experience trauma.

To prevent *the bad thing* from happening again, many of us with unhealed trauma living in our nervous systems learn to sever from the wisdom of our bodies. We become hypervigilant and trapped in a state of defensive orienting. Over time this hardwires our nervous systems for prioritizing the tracking of danger over the tracking of nourishment, safety, connection, and love. Therefore, part of learning to recalibrate your inner compass is learning to give voice to, trust, and to follow the instincts of your body and its powerful sensory system.

As you explore using your senses to recalibrate your inner compass, notice if one sense feels easier and provides more feedback than any of the others. As human beings, we frequently have a dominant sense that can become a part of our personal resources.

Here are the guidelines for this practice:

1. **Choose a time to practice only when you find yourself feeling relatively safe** (i.e., not hauling down the highway at 75 mph, eating an energy bar, and listening to a podcast). Perhaps a moment of time alone, sitting outside (preferably) or near a window, with at least ten minutes to spare.

2. **When you are first learning about exploratory orienting, start by sitting or lying down.** You will find it much easier to actually drink in the world around you (especially if you aren't used to doing this) by reducing as much stimulation as possible from your body. Eventually, you can work your way up to walking or even hiking or running while you orient in an exploratory, pleasurable way.

3. **Once you have settled down and feel safe where you are, take a look around you.** What do you see? In your mind (or out loud), name what you see. Notice windows, light, clouds, and plant or animal life. Notice shapes, colors, and relationships between things (this is leaning on that, there is space between these things, etc.). Drink in your visual world as though for the first time. Ask yourself, *is there anything new and/or pleasurable to look at in my environment today?*

4. **Now, play with your auditory sense.** What do you hear? Do you hear the noises of nature? Noises from machinery? What noise is the closest? What noise is the farthest away? Is there a pattern or a rhythm to the noise? Or is it more random? Notice volume and also bass—are there any noises that you can also feel? If you can hear the sound of birds chirping, is it only one kind of bird chirping? Or are

there different kinds of birds chirping? Drink in your auditory world as though for the first time. Ask yourself, *is there anything new and/or pleasurable to listen to in my environment today?*

5. **Now, play with your sense of smell.** What do you smell? Do you smell anything distinctly, or is there a mixture of smells? Can you smell something close? What is the farthest thing you can smell? Drink in your olfactory information as though for the first time. Ask yourself, *is there anything new and/or pleasurable to smell in my environment today?*

6. **And finally, what do you feel?** This sense is a bit more complex, as feeling is an accumulation of information gathered in our physical bodies, in our psyches, and from previous associations with things. As much as you can, try to label what you feel in this present moment with sensations, such as coolness, warmth, stillness, energy, vibration, movement, stuck-ness, openness, tenderness, heaviness, lightness, softness, hardness, etc. Where do you feel these sensations? Do you feel them deep in your body? Or more on the surface? Do they center around a part of your body like an organ? Does this sensation bring with it any particular kind of emotion like grief, joy, anger, or hope? Drink in your feeling body as though for the first time. Ask yourself, *is there anything new and/or pleasurable that I am feeling at this moment?*

The feeling aspect of this exercise can bring up a lot for some of us. As much as you are able to stick with labeling sensations rather than stories—the better. Often our stories from the past hinder us from being able to actually feel what is happening in our bodies in the present. For example, if you have had a traumatic experience involving your reproductive organs such as a miscarriage, abortion, or medical or sexual abuse, when you are doing this exercise and you feel sensation there, it might feel alarming. Instead of exploring that sensation in the present moment, your psyche may take you directly to the story of the last experience you had with this part of your body. You may find yourself taken out of the present moment and traveling down the path of a previous, unhealed trauma response.

If you are sensing this might be your experience, or if you feel resistance to your body's sensations, feel free to modify this part of the invitation. You can skip it altogether if it feels too intense, or you can instead, work with an animal (horses and dogs are amazing with this work) and see if you can sense what they are feeling in their bodies, based on their movements. You can also do this with other healthy, safe humans, too, if you feel called. Try to practice exploratory orienting a little bit each day, even if you only have time for opening up to one sensory experience.

If you are used to defensive orienting, it may feel quite boring at first. This is only because your nervous system is more familiar with chaos and overstimulation than with pleasure and rest. But trust me, there are wonderful things happening underneath the surface that you will benefit from exponentially on your healing journey if you keep at it, such as:

+ Your nervous system is getting the memo that you are experiencing safety (woohoo!), perhaps for the first time in a long time.

+ Your nervous system is getting this experience of safety repeated over and over again—as often as you can make space for this exercise. This creates new and healthy patterns for your nervous system to track rather than the habitual ones that led you astray.

+ You are using the wisdom of your body and its multitude of senses rather than just your eyes, which can sometimes be locked in a state of hypervigilant tracking.

✦ You are likely breathing more healthfully when you are practicing exploratory orienting because your nervous system is staying in a parasympathetic, rest and digest state.

✦ You are creating a new relationship with your body, opening up to its powerful sensory system, and receiving feedback from the environment.

✦ You are opening your nervous system to experiencing and savoring good things like slowness, spaciousness, and pleasure.

✦ You are opening your psyche to experiencing and savoring good things like nourishment, safety, connection, playfulness, and love.

✦ You are expanding your window of tolerance.

✦ You are increasing your bandwidth for sensation.

✦ You are learning to come more into the present moment, which is healing in and of itself, as trauma often keeps us trapped in the past or stuck trying to predict the future.

Once you feel you have gotten the hang of it, try practicing this while in motion, such as during a walk or hike or while wading in the ocean. See if you are able to track what sensory information you are receiving while also receiving feedback from the stimulation of moving your body. This is the *ultimate* in multitasking. I like to practice exploratory orienting when I have natural moments of pause, such as while sitting in an office waiting to be called on for an appointment or going on a walk with my dogs. It is also incredibly useful after you have experienced something stressful, but only after you have registered that you are now in a safe place and the stressful event is over.

Recalibrating your inner compass will strengthen your intuition, and your intuition will keep you safe, guide you in your decisions big and small, as well as keep you and your actions aligned with your most authentic self. Intuition is like a muscle and you can strengthen it with use or cause it to atrophy by not using it. The keys to strengthening your intuition lie in strengthening your relationship with your body through your senses, taking action based on your *hunches*, and reflecting on how these actions have served (or not served) you, reflecting back for accuracy in your hunches. Ask yourself, "Was my intuition correct?"

As a being who is born from and belongs to the Earth, I hope you can *feel* how powerful your sensory system is. To sever from this part of yourself is to sever from one of your greatest resources: your body and its wisdom. To regain this power will enable you to repair some of the damage caused by trauma and to learn to trust yourself once again to become the wise, grounded, fully embodied being that you are. If you keep doing your personal trauma-tending work, trust that your intuition will grow to be more and more efficient and dependable over time. Add your powerful hunter-gatherer sensory system and intuition to your list of personal resources and practice using it throughout our work together in the following pages.

CHAPTER FOUR:

BOUNDARIES AS AN ESSENTIAL SURVIVAL SKILL

OUR HUNTER-GATHERER ANCESTORS survived not only because they were highly intuitive but also because they lived within and could rely on their communities. I have learned from many years of working amongst *Indigenous* communities of Nepal, Tibet, North America, Thailand, and Burma that there is no such thing as a separate individual. People are seen as a part of the matrix of a larger community, so much so that their identities often include not only family names but also tribal or community names. Even the names of local flora, fauna, as well as features of the landscape were often seen as part of their identities. "I am so-and-so from the so-and-so community of such-and-such place," is not an uncommon way to introduce oneself in these communities.

What does it mean to be Indigenous or from an Indigenous community? In general, Indigenous peoples are descendants of those who inhabited a region at the time people of different cultures or ethnic origins arrived. Those who newly arrived in the region became dominant through conquest, occupation, settlement, enslavement, genocide, and colonization. Indigenous people are people practicing unique traditions, retaining social, cultural, economic, and political characteristics that differ from the dominant societies in which they currently live.

Because, historically, our hunter-gatherer ancestors relied on their families and communities for safety and food; it was vital to develop the social and emotional skills needed to function within a community; going it alone was almost certain death. In hunter-gatherer communities, it was common for individuals to contribute to the needs and wellness of the larger community, and even babies were nursed by several mothers enabling new mothers to get rest or to tend to other work. This was not a utopia of neighborly love, rather this was a way to share the workload that required staying in relationships with other humans.

In America, what used to be community culture is now a culture built on the false notion of individualism. Our modern, American vision of family has become the nuclear family—parents and the child or children without the presence of aunts, uncles, grandmothers, and grandfathers or other important ancestors. Not only this, nuclear families are now responsible for pulling weight in all the departments: earning an income, raising a family, caring for other family members, keeping up a house and/or property, etc., and not only is this causing significant stress, but it is also causing us and our children to lose our relational skills with other humans. The ability to relate in a healthy way with other humans requires essential communication skills, and most especially, the ability to communicate our boundaries.

What is a *boundary*? A boundary is a physical and/or energetic buffer that separates you from your world. Boundaries are both real and perceived, tangible and intangible. One real and tangible boundary is your skin, for example. It holds all of your organs within it and keeps the contents of the world outside of it (except, of course, for our nostrils, which bring air into our lungs and our mouths, which bring nourishment into our bellies). Another tangible boundary is that of a lake shoreline—under normal conditions, this boundary keeps the water in the lake and the land around the lake dry.

An example of a perceived and intangible boundary are boundaries you set for yourself. If, like most humans, you want to live, you will have an intangible boundary that will have the effect of not letting you step over a cliff edge without the proper equipment. Most of us know not to walk into a store without our clothes on, which is another example of a perceived boundary. Most of us know it is not okay to walk up to a complete stranger and touch them, which is a perceived boundary.

Boundaries are everywhere. When yours are good and clear, they will make you feel safe. Others also feel safe with you when you have good boundaries. If you know where my boundaries are, then you can better feel your own boundaries. If, on the other hand, you aren't sure where my boundaries are, it might be more difficult for you to feel your own. You need to have boundaries with the culture and with other beings. You may or may not want others to talk to you a certain way or to touch you. Having a boundary enables you to let the other being know what type of contact you are up for and what type you aren't.

Healthy boundaries are rather fluid; they flex and bend as our needs arise and morph. Boundaries indicate who and where we are in space. They illustrate our "yes" from our "no." They can act as an inner compass, orienting and guiding us toward health. With healthy boundaries, we can enter into a state of feeling deeply connected to and a part of the world around us all the while staying in contact with our sense of self. This can serve as a gateway to experience what is often referred to as a non-dual state of consciousness where we can momentarily diffuse our sense of self and merge energetically with the world around us without losing ourselves in the process. Many spiritual and religious traditions around the world recognize this state of unity and incorporate its wisdom into their teachings.

On the other hand, when boundaries are not fluid and are instead rigid, they can hinder us by locking us into a dual state of consciousness—placing a perceived vast chasm between us and our world. A dual state of consciousness creates the "self" and "other" paradigm with which we have become so familiar.

Don't get me wrong—sometimes this is needed. Many of us, especially in the innocence of our youth, walk around with relatively diffuse boundaries.

We are naturally inclined to walk the Earth with our hearts on our sleeves simply because it feels so good to feel this deep and authentic connection. But then, one day, life throws us a curveball, and we experience something traumatic. After trauma (which always includes some type of boundary violation), we often need to repair our boundaries and that repair frequently includes becoming *over-bounded* for a period of time, as this will make us feel safer. To be over-bounded is to have inflexible boundaries that are formed not only to serve as a barrier from potential future negative experiences, but can also inadvertently create a barrier for positive ones, too.

I once had a client named Maggie who had a trauma response to an experience at a chiropractor's office many years prior to having met her, leaving her in an over-bounded state. Maggie was a creative, introverted, highly empathic woman in her sixties who lost both her mother and her husband (two of her primary supports) to chronic health issues only a year prior to the incident. What happened at the chiropractor's office was a combination of Maggie's fragile bones after years of managing osteoporosis, with too strong a force from the chiropractor, and Maggie's clavicle fractured during the adjustment. As if that wasn't scary enough, when she expressed having severe pain on and around her clavicle after the adjustment, the chiropractor told her she was being overly sensitive and to go home and ice it. She left quietly and in tears, driving herself to urgent care only to discover that she was in fact, correct. Her clavicle had fractured not in one place, but in two.

Not surprisingly, she had a trauma response to this experience, and even years later, each time she came to my office for acupuncture, it didn't matter how kind or nurturing I was or how gentle the treatment was— she was frequently short-tempered and angry, not allowing in any of the nourishment I, or my staff were offering. Her fight trauma response— which was due to the loss of control and dismissiveness of her feelings at the chiropractor's office—was immediately triggered simply by being in a medical office. It didn't matter what I did or said. I knew she was afraid, and I could not take her lack of trust personally. It wasn't until after two years of building rapport with her that her boundaries softened (and her tight muscles did, too), and she began to open up and let me see the incredible, artistic, and deeply compassionate person she truly was underneath all the trauma responses. One time she even brought me flowers from the farmer's market! That's when I knew she was really healing.

When we become over-bounded, the longer we stay on our side of the chasm reinforcing the *us versus them* dynamic. Ultimately, we become more isolated and isolation leads to more feelings of separateness, and then separation breeds fear. This is something I see happening frequently after trauma; people become over-bounded in response to the experience(s) and then get stuck there, which only heightens the fear. It can be easy, for example, once we have experienced a boundary violation from another human, to have a backlash of withdrawing from or becoming hypercritical of our relationships with other humans.

People who identify as highly empathic, frequently have to work harder at boundaries because it is in their nature to be slightly under-bounded, which leaves them more vulnerable to others' energies (but when honed, this can lead them to become extremely perceptive, making them excellent healers among other professions where reading between the lines is pertinent).

And yet, *we need boundaries* because we don't want to live at the mercy of our world nor our thoughts. We also don't want to live at the mercy of other people, and their thoughts of us. Without boundaries, we would walk off cliffs, think it's okay to touch strangers, and otherwise not have a clear sense of ourselves. We would merge dangerously with others, placing our lives and psyches at risk of further traumatization, which of course many people who have experienced trauma often do.

We deal with boundary violations every single day in the West (and many other places around the world) with the pollution of our air, toxins leaching into our water, and the many chemicals found in our food. These violations require that we stay vigilant so that we can stay safe. Marches, rallies, and protests are common responses to boundary violations.

We are all guilty of violating the boundaries of others. We frequently take Earth's resources without asking and without reciprocity or gratitude. Many of our ancestors have colonized other countries, a huge boundary violation. Childhood abuse (and any kind of abuse) is a boundary violation. Treating the drinking water of large communities with toxic chemicals is a boundary violation. There are boundary violations that happen in the medical field every day, including not listening to patients, over- or under-prescribing procedures or medications. And the list goes on.

One boundary violation that occurs almost daily is that of pacing and stimulation. Many of us feel trapped having to move too fast, expected to answer too many calls or emails and take on far more than we are able to process and integrate at any given time. This is why I tell my patients and students that learning to set a boundary by slowing things down and reducing stimulation is the greatest single act of rebellion against a culture that rewards those who can *go with the flow*. Why? Because when you begin to slow things down, you begin to actually *feel things*. You begin to feel more of who you are, you begin to hear your own voice instead of the voices of others, you begin to repair your relationship with your intuition, and you begin to feel a natural sense of empowerment and belonging that is not dependent on outside influences or consumerism. And for a culture that profits from the status quo, this is the greatest threat.

Despite our challenge with setting boundaries for ourselves, some of us struggle more with being over-bounded (this is very common during a freeze response). Our over-boundedness is what leads us to become stuck in a dual state of consciousness, unable to access feelings of unity. I believe this is why some humans are drawn to substances that alter consciousness and dissolve boundaries, specifically psychedelics. Currently, psychedelics are making a comeback and even becoming decriminalized in many states. Many of us are tired of feeling so separate, so much so that we are seeking comfort through the plant and fungus kingdom, which can support us into feeling more a part of the life around us and less separate. Plants like ayahuasca, peyote, coca, salvia, cannabis, poppy, and mushrooms such as those containing psilocybin all have an incredible ability to numb the parts of our brain that tell us *we are separate beings,* mostly the prefrontal cortex but also the anterior and posterior cingulate cortex (1). This can lead to experiencing a non-dual state of unity with the world. As non-Indigenous people who are more familiar with living in a world that encourages separateness, this state can feel wildly comforting and also liberating.

Though if you are in a resource deficit, with significant unhealed trauma living in your nervous system, entering this non-dual state through the use of psychedelics can be, in and of itself, traumatic. Without the psychological safety that boundaries provide for you, you could wind up feeling extremely vulnerable and scared. However, with a well-trained guide, we are learning that this experience could in fact become healing (2). There are therapists trained to support their clients in healing from trauma through experiences like this with the help of substances like ketamine, ayahuasca, psilocybin, and methylenedioxymethamphetamine (MDMA). If this type of healing work is calling to you, consider discussing this with your therapist or other support professionals.

Ingested substances aren't the only things that can bring you into this space of oneness. Meditation, prayer, ritual, ceremony, chanting, the scent of burning herbs or oils, fasting, receiving acupuncture and/or bodywork, and other practices can bring you there, too. Near-death experiences and close calls can also, inadvertently, take you right to that non-dual terrain (not that I am recommending them as a pathway to experience oneness because these experiences can create trauma responses, too). The experience of immense grief also has the power to bring you into a non-dual state. Have you ever lost someone close to you and that loss has left you tender, raw, open, and feeling more connected to others and to life than ever before?

Since trauma always includes some type of boundary violation, as a consequence we lose our ability to set boundaries. We have difficulty saying "no," and when we can't say "no," our "yes" carries zero weight. Just think about your relationship with conflict. Many of us are conflict avoidant because our ability to set or negotiate boundaries is limited. Even though conflict can bring up a threat response, conflict is simply: *my boundary bumped up against your boundary.* When we don't have the skills to navigate conflict, we wind up forgoing our own personal boundaries and walking through the world feeling unsafe. So, how do we restore a sense of safety back inside of ourselves?

AN INVITATION:
Restoring the Shoreline

Like a river cascading through the forest, the shoreline serves as a boundary protecting both the river and the forest. The soil, rocks, sand, and tree roots literally hold the Earth in, providing an important boundary for water. You must learn to be river-like when the water is safe and nourishing and to be forest-like when it is not; this creates healthy boundaries.

To better understand how you operate in the world and the kind of space you need to feel safe, I invite you to begin examining where your boundaries naturally live and to learn to grow wider boundaries when needed. Are they strong and clear? Are they murky and diffused? Do you hold stronger boundaries with people than with the natural world? Can you tighten up your boundaries when it is not safe, and can you soften them when it is?

Let's play with this a little bit, okay? When you are able, set aside about an hour when you can ideally be outside or, at the very least, inside a large room. You will also need a long piece of rope of at least twelve feet but no more than twenty feet. Any kind of rope is fine as long as you feel comfortable having it on the ground or floor.

1. **Stand or sit in the center of your space.** Start this exercise standing, if possible, or sitting in a chair or on the ground if needed.

2. **Make a circle.** Take your rope and make a circle with it in front of you that is about one foot in diameter. Step inside the circle.

3. **Imagine this circle represents your boundary.** Fill this perceived boundary with your energy so that you take up as much space as your boundary will allow. Using your intuition, how does it feel to have a boundary that is one foot in diameter? What do you notice in your body? Does it feel free? Or constrained? Does it feel safe? Or unsafe?

4. **Grow your space.** Step out of the circle and now, take your rope and widen it so that it creates about twice as large a circle as before. Step back in the circle.

5. **Fill this perceived boundary with your energy.** Take up as much space as your rope boundary will allow. Using your intuition, how does a boundary this size feel? What do you notice in your body? Does it feel more free? Or constrained? Does it feel more safe? Or unsafe? What would it feel like to wander the world with a boundary this size?

6. **Grow your space again.** Step out of the circle and now, take your rope and widen it so it creates about twice as large a circle as before. It should be about four feet in diameter at this point. Step back in the circle.

7. **Fill this perceived boundary with even more of your energy.** Take up as much space as your boundary will allow. Using your intuition, how does a boundary this size feel? What do you notice in your body? Does it feel more free? Or constrained? Does it feel more safe? Or unsafe? What would it feel like to wander the world with a boundary this size?

8. **Keep widening your perceived boundary using the rope.** Feel what it feels like to have a safe space inside the physical representation of your boundary. Each time you widen your circle, give yourself permission to take up that much more space. Using your intuition,

ask yourself, where do you find the greatest resonance? Where do you feel the safest? The most freedom? I realize you may even want a larger boundary than the rope you are using! Go get more rope and play with it until it feels just right in your nervous system.

9. **Take an internal snapshot.** When you are ready, take a snapshot with your eyes and your felt sense and go ahead and remove the rope boundary. Can you maintain that boundary without the visual representation? Can you still fill that much space?

10. **Go for a walk with your boundary.** With this ideal boundary diameter held in your mind's eye, I want you to take a walk. Walk slowly and see if you can keep some of your awareness on this perceived boundary. Allow your body to take up as much space as your boundary will allow. Feel what it feels like to take up space inside a perceived boundary.

This exercise should give you some information about yourself: where your boundaries typically exist and where they need to be so that you can feel safe and empowered. Many of us are conditioned from a young age to take up as little space as possible. This is part of some of the collective trauma that we have all inherited. What is it like to be invited to take up so much space as your circle grows and grows? Were you able to? Or did you find that there was a limit to how much space you were able to take up? What is it like to walk through the world in this way? Can you grow your sense of self to become the size of a house? The size of a city block? How much space can you energetically take up? And can you hold it?

The information you gather in this exercise will give you insight into your natural boundaries and how they relate to your sense of self. Typically, when your sense of self is small, you will also have more diffused boundaries. However, as your sense of self grows during your healing work, your boundaries can also grow stronger. Eventually, you can find yourself able to take up appropriate space while feeling safe and contained within your personal boundaries. Practice this exercise, especially when you are feeling more vulnerable. Consider using the rope if you need the physical representation to regain that internal sense of safety as you navigate the world/this material.

AN INVITATION:
Hard Eyes, Soft Eyes

Now that you have explored what it feels like to have solid, wide boundaries that allow you and your nervous system to experience safety as you navigate the world, let's play with hardening and softening those boundaries so that you can experience *flexibility*. One way to practice this is to play with your visual sense.

As Westerners, we are trained to see the world through *hard eyes*—the eyes of a hunter who must study their prey with their eyes to gain accurate information. Of course, there is wisdom to this ability. As someone well-traveled, when I have found myself alone in foreign places, I frequently need to have on my hard eyes. They keep me on the lookout for potential threats and this keeps me safe.

However, the problem with having full-time hard eyes is that it can lock you into a state of duality, creating a rigid boundary and a constant feeling of separateness. Then, sometime later, when you are actually safe and welcome to relax and soften your boundary, it can become difficult to do this. This is also what happens when we are stuck in a trauma state. As we have learned, getting stuck in a trauma state takes our awareness from fluidly moving from the inner landscape to the outer landscape and back again—to suddenly leaving us stuck tracking the outer landscape only. In this state, we become hypervigilant and oriented mostly to see threats in the environment rather than seeing goodness. Not to mention, while we are giving so much weight to our visual field with hard eyes, our other powerful senses have been forced to take a backseat.

Hard eyes are the opposite of *soft eyes*. To have soft eyes means you are not prioritizing one sense over another. Rather, you are plugged into the wisdom and feedback loops of your entire body and its sensory system. To have soft eyes means you are seeing, hearing, smelling, and feeling all at about the same level of intensity. Having soft eyes enables you to experience some degree of non-duality due to having more flexible boundaries. This gatherer skill will give you access to a thousand times more information about your inner and outer landscape than if you were to prioritize only one sense.

I want to introduce you to one of my favorite practices for working with boundaries; I call it *Hard Eyes, Soft Eyes.*

1. **Find a comfortable and safe place to sit, stand, or lie down.** Take a few deep breaths to help you more fully arrive. Try some plant breathing if that feels resonant.

2. **Notice your inner landscape.** What is happening there today? Is it quiet and still, or chaotic and rambunctious? What kinds of emotions are in there? What stories are you hearing? Notice without judgment.

3. **Notice your outer landscape.** What is happening there today? Take a look around you. What colors do you see? What shapes, patterns, or objects are present? What relationships between objects? If this is a familiar place for you, has anything about it changed? Look at the edges of objects and the spaces between them. Notice what you are drawn to look at and what you may have an aversion to. Study your environment, and take note of what it's like to do this. These are your hard eyes turning on.

4. **Take a break.** Once you have practiced turning on your hard eyes for at least two minutes, take a break. If you'd like, you can even step away for a moment or change your position. Give yourself a moment to process what happened for you during that interaction. Were you able to gather any information from your body or other senses?

5. **Turn on your soft eyes.** As if you are allowing your eyes to sink far into the back of your head, begin gazing into your environment. This should allow you to open up your peripheral vision, similar to looking at one of those Magic Eye Pictures. Keep your eyes from opening all the way, and instead of fixating your vision on the objects, look softly at the horizon, allowing everything in between you and the horizon to become a one, united image. Practice this for two minutes and blink as much as you need to.

6. **Turn your attention inward.** After at least two minutes of practicing soft eyes, notice what you are feeling in your body while you are gazing at the horizon. Are you feeling soft and open? Are you feeling warm or cool? Are you feeling anxious or weepy? Are you still breathing? Only notice.

7. **Take a break.** Once you have noticed your inner landscape while gazing at the horizon, close your eyes and take a break. If you'd like, you can even step away for a moment or change your position.

8. **Notice what you gathered from your sensory system.** Were you able to gather any information from your body or other senses? What were you hearing while practicing soft eyes? What were you smelling? What were you feeling? If you'd like, you can spend some time going back and forth between hard eyes and soft eyes, noting any differences between the two experiences. Consider journaling for a moment to draw out these differences.

Typically when we practice hard eyes, we become more critical, judgmental, our hearts close down, our minds race, we breathe more shallowly, feel more anxious and cold, and our muscles clench—frequently our jaw and temporal muscles. This is because hard eyes entice a more rigid boundary in our psyche and nervous system.

And when we practice soft eyes, we often feel exactly the opposite. We feel relaxed in our bodies, our hearts open, our minds calm, we feel connected, we feel receptive and warm, and we breathe more deeply. This is because soft eyes entice more flexible boundaries in our psyche and nervous system.

If and when you feel ready, I recommend practicing hard eyes, soft eyes with yourself in the mirror and also with other humans and animals to see what additional information you can gain about your boundaries, including what feels more comfortable to you. Boundaries not only protect your physical body, but they also protect your energy and give you access to feelings of safety no matter where or with who you find yourself. Are there other boundaries you have noticed are missing in your life and in your relationships? Are there boundaries that feel excessive and out of alignment? Are there boundaries that need renegotiating in one relationship or another?

As we move into Part Two and begin unpacking some of your history and the history of your ancestors, see if you can find a boundary that keeps you feeling open, yet safe, flexible, yet grounded. You will know if you have succeeded because your nervous system will remain regulated with your interoception turned on, even while traversing challenging terrain. And, if you *do* find yourself becoming dysregulated, dissociating, or fragmenting, you will be more likely to notice and come back home more quickly.

As human beings on the healing journey, the ability to be flexible, setting, holding, and shifting boundaries as needed is an essential life skill. This is not only to keep us safe in our world, but it also supports us relationally. In our postmodern world, while it may appear as though we don't need other humans, we do. We may not need them for the same reasons our ancestors needed other humans (for food and fending off prey). We need them for a number of other reasons that we will dive into later.

INTERLUDE

FOR MOST OF US, we don't begin our work of tending to our unhealed trauma responses until we have reached a boiling point where we cannot function in the same way as before. We rarely tend to our trauma—not because we don't want to, but rather perhaps because we didn't even realize how much our lives have been impacted by the traumas of our past. Maybe we masked our trauma responses with productivity, or maybe we fragmented and went numb. Some of us don't even realize that we are carrying trauma around with us until we notice how many of the choices we thought we were making out of free will turned out to be trauma responses—the beginning or ending of certain relationships or careers, addictions, and even the type of work and play we have engaged in. Often when we connect these dots, we discover a freight truck full of trauma responses and unmet needs.

Tending trauma is not for the faint of heart, nor is it as readily available for those without privilege. It takes significant time, energy, and resources. Even with resources, many of us won't go near our unhealed trauma until we are in a crisis and life stops us dead in our tracks, when we have no other option but to look inward, at ourselves, and at our life's choices. The following story is about how life stopped me dead in my tracks and forced me to look inward at the residue of trauma I mistakenly thought I had healed from long ago.

Sitting on an airplane about to fly home to Colorado after many long months of travel and work both nationally and internationally, I had one of the most frightening experiences of my life as I awoke to witnessing myself going blind, one growing black spot in my vision at a time. From the outside, it seemed to come out of nowhere. Though I know nature is not that unkind. There were so many warning signs I ignored along the way. Life was preparing me to cross a threshold into darkness, literally and figuratively. But I didn't just wake up blind on that plane; let me back up a moment and give you some context.

Since 2013 I had been running an international nonprofit and traveling twice each year for weeks (and sometimes months) at a time. We were leading teams of volunteers into the most impoverished communities around the world and hosting medical clinics. In the foothills of the Rocky Mountains, I also had a full-time women's health specialty private practice with staff where I saw eight to twelve patients each day, five days a week. My partner and I were rescuing and rehabilitating dogs—specifically, bully breeds from shelters that euthanize them without cause. Life was b-u-s-y—though, in truth—I loved everything I was doing. It was just that the wheels never really stopped spinning. *I was flying under my own highly trained radar.*

I was on the plane that day because I had been invited to speak at a predominantly black high school for poor and at-risk youth, *my* former high school in fact. They wanted me to come and talk to the graduating class about how I got from where they were (at the mercy of so many oppressive systems) to where I was at "now" (apparently free from those systems and living my best life). They saw me as successful—and I could see why they would be so inclined. It is easy to put women who present like me on a pedestal. I appear highly functional, I look well put together, and I have a bustling resume.

Little did they know I had come from nothing: a poor, broken, uneducated family on welfare and food stamps, and a single mother who struggled immensely with drug- and alcohol-addiction. I learned to survive the hard way—by waking each day and taking life as it comes. I am under no illusions that it was a damn miracle I was able to create a life so different from my family's.

The high school I went to was known for being the place where "troubled" kids go. Even though I was super smart, I was also a major rebel. I could see through the bs of our educational system and had little to no respect for so-called authority. Because I needed to take care of myself and start building my own personal financial resources, I had also held a job since I was fourteen.

There was, after all, no one to catch me, or my brother, if I fell.

Out of necessity, on any given day I would easily prioritize working and earning money over attending school. In my first year of the first high school I attended—which was rural and white—I skipped more days than I attended and was even put in juvenile detention one summer for truancy (and smoking cigarettes and running away from home, and all the naughty teenage things).

I always smelled like a mixture of pot and cigarette smoke, and when they randomly brought the drug dogs in to sniff lockers, mine was *always* the one they stopped at. While I certainly smelled like drugs, they had no clue that it wasn't because of my own pot smoking. But for that reason alone, smelling like drugs got me suspended more times than I can count. Yet at the end of the school year, I still somehow always had straight A's.

I am grateful for my guidance counselor at this school, who sensed (at least somewhat) what I was up against at home. She found a high school program that would enable me to keep my job and work through the curriculum at my own pace—Virginia Randolph High School, the first all-black high school in the history of Virginia. They had a program called *The Center for Diversified Studies,* and it was made for students like me. I didn't know it at the time, but I was to become the youngest student ever to be allowed in. The program set you up so that you could go as fast through a traditional high school curriculum as you needed to, and at the end of the day, you would still get a high school diploma. And as you can imagine, I needed to go *fast*.

I managed to keep a near-full-time job while I attended my new high school, and halfway through my final year, I had the school bus drop me off at a used car dealership, where I bought my first car with my own saved money, a 1991 Chevrolet Cavalier painted kelly green and with gold spray-painted rims.

Once I had my car, I completed a year of dual enrollment in a local college, and graduated from high school at sixteen with all A's and a year of college credit under my belt. I packed my bags and immediately moved into a cockroach-infested, third-floor apartment in downtown Richmond, Virginia, one block from the homeless shelter and three blocks from the bus station. It was a dream come true for me—seriously. I was free. I adopted an eighty-pound pit bull named Orion to keep me safe. But then I knew I really couldn't falter. Failure for me at that point would have meant living on the streets. I worked three jobs and hustled my way into my early twenties, and that was when I think I took my first real breath.

So, this was me on the plane that morning years later, heading home after speaking at my old high school in an attempt to inspire these young people. Yet I, myself, was still in survival mode, unwilling to admit it. With my hyper-aroused nervous system, I was exhausted and playing out the trauma from my childhood well into adulthood, I was beyond disconnected from my body and from the Earth. I had no boundaries and no sense of self. I was simply reacting to my life.

It was apparent I had this kind of urgency set in me from a young age. I think it came to me twofold; from losing my dad in an accident at the young age of nine, which taught me never to trust anything and that accidents, sickness, and death can happen to any of us at any time, *so be prepared*. If you have also had this experience, then you know it's like waiting for the other shoe to drop, *constantly*.

I also think this behavior was set in me from having a childhood where simply getting through the day relatively unscathed was the goal. In the depths of my psyche, I felt that as long as I was hustling, I would never again be at the mercy of having to depend on others. I knew that if I faltered in life—*there was nowhere to return to*. I had to make it or else.

On the plane that morning, as I was coming down from all the public speaking, I ordered a coffee—something I usually only turn to when I'm exhausted and burned out—and sat back to have some small talk with my row-mate. That's when I noticed something strange: the vision in my left eye was somewhat blurry, almost as if something was floating in the center of my eye. I tried rubbing my eyelid to clear it up, whatever it was. But it stayed there right smack in the middle of my vision. I tried to forget about it and put my chair back to drink my coffee and look out the window.

Then suddenly, I noticed that the vision in my left eye was becoming distorted. As I was looking around the plane, lines that were supposed to be straight were suddenly curved—almost as if I was looking through a fishbowl. I was getting pretty freaked out and asked my row-mate if he wouldn't mind getting up so I could go to the bathroom. While in the tiny, cramped bathroom with shaky, spotty lighting and motion sickness coming at me in waves, I studied my eye in the mirror, and it looked normal from the outside. I couldn't find anything floating or noticeably irritating. I washed my face with soap and water to try to freshen up. *Was I trapped inside a bad dream? Was I about to go blind? Or have some sort of neurological episode like a stroke?*

I went back to my seat and sat down to try to do some meditating and breathing, and any other self-resourcing tools I could conjure up. The truth was, I was feeling really anxious and scared, my heart nearly beating out of its chest. I closed my eyes for a moment and took a few deep breaths. When I opened my eyes, all of a sudden, instead of just a distorted place in my vision, I now had a large black spot in the center of my vision in my left eye. I was looking around the plane and could only see the periphery in my left eye. I was officially panicking.

I turned to the gentleman next to me and told him what was happening. I wanted him to know in case something terrible happened to me on the plane and I wasn't able to see or speak for myself. He was very kind and also optimistic that maybe it had something to do with the altitude and would resolve when we landed. I thought—perhaps he is right—and tried to settle down and keep my cool. Inside, I was the farthest thing from calm. I mean, at that point, I had trekked for many years through the Himalayas and the Rockies—getting well above 13,000 and 14,000 feet. I had never had trouble with altitude before, so why would I be having it now?

For someone like me, who is highly functional and self-sufficient *to the extreme*, to be incapacitated and therefore become dependent on another human being is and will always be my greatest challenge. According to my unconscious, feeling helpless equals certain death.

What started as distortion and a small black spot in my vision grew to near-blindness in my left eye while on the plane. I was terrified, and as soon as we landed, I called my eye doctor to let them know what was happening. They wanted to see me immediately. My eye doctor took one look at my eye using their high-tech equipment and quickly referred me to a specialist the next town over. With my partner behind the wheel, we flew down the highway, my legs shaking and my mind thinking the worst: *I'm going to go blind. I've been pushing too hard. I haven't taken enough time off. I'm being punished. My life, as I know it—is over. What did I do to deserve this? Was it abandoning my mom in the throes of her addiction? Was it leaving my brother behind so that the military became his only safe-ish place to go? Have I just seen too much in this life? Was it because my life and my vision got too big for someone like me? Had I simply experienced too much trauma?* (Stay tuned as this story continues in the next interlude . . . .)

This was my breaking point. The truth was, even knowing everything that I knew about psychology and trauma, even though I had developed enormous resources in my life and had come so far, I had lost my way and was living at the mercy of my unhealed trauma running rampant in my nervous system. I was completely disconnected from my body and from the Earth, what would have been incredible healing resources for me.

I know from many years in private practice that as humans we are incredibly tolerant and resilient—I witness it every single day. We learn to move forward despite all odds, despite balls and chains dragging behind us, despite two broken, bleeding legs, *we will walk on*. There is no doubt in my mind of our strength and enormous capacity for challenge and hardship. And yet, so often by the time we are seeking support for whatever is happening in our bodies and in our psyches, the challenges we face have reached a boiling point where we cannot function in the same way as before (which was often unrealistic to begin with). And sadly, it is the loss of functioning—and not the challenge itself—that leads us to our breaking point.

I knew I was not alone. So many of us are chugging along in the same train car, having bought into a misaligned paradigm, waiting until we reach a breaking point in our lives where we simply can't go on with the way things are. Often these breaking points include a health crisis or a single or series of life-altering events that stop us dead in our tracks—beckoning for us to wake up (betrayal, divorce, death, miscarriage or loss of a child, loss of a job, etc.).

Being vulnerable to cultural programming and to what we deem as "normal" in a particular society is a symptom that is exacerbated by unhealed trauma and a consequential loss of connection to ourselves and with the Earth, our greatest resources as human beings. My ability to *buy into* the "shoulds" laid on to me by the culture was made possible by those early experiences that told me I wasn't good enough, that I didn't belong, and that I was going to need to prove myself if I were to succeed. That fear, that shaky ground, provided the very fuel to keep me moving at such an unrealistic pace. Even though I had learned so much about myself and my own trauma, my nervous system was still stuck in a trauma response.

According to my mind, keeping that high-stress lifestyle and fast pace in adulthood was just plain silly—perhaps even re-traumatizing. But according to my nervous system, it was just familiar terrain. The predator was no longer any one person but rather had become society and its messaging and pressures as a whole—and in response, I was fawning. I was doing all the things that the culture was telling me to do so that I could find supposed happiness and freedom from scarcity: work, participate, and do something good in the world. I was unprepared for this—blindsided by the consequences of taking on so much. Though it never felt like too much to me because my nervous system had learned to have such a great capacity for stress. But that was the unhealed trauma talking that was still living in my nervous system—and it wasn't something to celebrate.

PART TWO:

PERSONAL, ANCESTRAL, AND COLLECTIVE TRAUMA

"Sometimes this broken heart gives birth to anxiety, and panic, sometimes to anger, resentment, and blame. But under the hardness of that armor there is a tenderness of genuine sadness. This is our link with all those who have ever loved."

—Pema Chodron

GIVEN THE BRILLIANCE and resilience of humanity, how did we wind up here in so much trouble? Where did we go wrong that so many of us on the planet are so traumatized and do not feel like we belong to the very body, the family, or the planet from which we are born? In Part Two, we're going to do some unpacking to see how we got here. We will shine a light into the dark corners of your ancestral and collective wounding. We will dive into attachment, limbic imprinting, and take a look at how trauma gets passed down from generation to generation as well as held in the collective field. You will be invited to put some pieces of your puzzle together as I guide you through crafting your psychological family tree. You will uncover and explore how you (and all of us) became so disconnected from ourselves, one another, and the Earth and what might be holding you back from your own healing.

CHAPTER FIVE:

PERSONAL TRAUMA AND ATTACHMENT WOUNDS

A NOTE OF GENTLENESS: As we dive into this terrain together, I am going to invite you to see your life and your challenges in a new way that risks cracking the foundation of some stories you have been telling yourself, perhaps for your whole life (and the stories you have been told by others). In this dissolution, you will be forced to let go of some things. You might be ready to let go of some of these stories or aspects of your identity. But others might catch you by surprise. You may fracture the very identity you have so carefully crafted for yourself. In this unraveling, you may feel a little bit shaky, a little bit uncertain, and you may need to pause and return to some practices from Part One. You may want to turn back. Hold yourself and your process gently, and take all the time you need for this leg of the journey. In the fracturing, the light will finally have a place to shine through.

It comes as no surprise that, as children, we are 100 percent immersed in and dependent on the nervous systems of the adults who set the emotional environment that we grow up in. The care that is provided to us (or not provided to us) will give us our psychological foundation (or lack thereof) for the rest of our lives. In psychology, we call this foundation *attachment*.

Attachment includes not only attachment to other humans but also basic attachment to life, to our bodies, and to the Earth. Attachment is important if we are to access feelings of safety and belonging in both childhood and adulthood. Attachment allows for bonding to develop and when we have *secure* attachment, we will become more resilient and have a strong foundation for the full spectrum of our human experience.

The opposite is also true when we have an insecure attachment. Attachment wounds underpin much of our personal traumas and they can spearhead significant personal challenges for us well into adulthood. They are like a crack in the foundation, greatly impacting our ability to feel our authenticity and to sense our innate belonging.

Attachment includes developing what is called a *secure base*. A secure base for an infant is typically the mother or primary caregiver. Think of this like a tetherball: the stable pole in the middle representing the caregiver who has become a secure base, and you being represented by the ball attached to the pole by the rope. When, as children, you are securely attached to your base, you will feel safe enough to explore your world precisely because your attachment tethers you to your secure base. As you become older, your secure base enables you to stretch your rope further and further because you trust you have that secure base to come back to.

As infants, we are wired for survival, and therefore, we have to learn to develop strategies to ensure that this attachment happens. This is true for all babies, even babies who have the most magical, welcoming conception, birth, and entry into a loving and present family. These survival strategies are called attachment styles and were initially formulated by John Bowlby in 1949 and first published in *Attachment and Loss, Volume One in 1969* (1).

According to this theory, which has now been widely adopted by the World Health Organization (2) and those practicing psychology around the world, when you are an infant, you have the ability to develop either a secure attachment or an insecure attachment with your caregiver. *This adoption will lead to a lifetime of either health and relationship-promoting behaviors or a lack of health and challenging relationships with yourself and the outside world.*

When babies are in utero, not only are they literally inside the nervous system field of their mother, but they are also engulfed in their mother's *biochemistry*. The term biochemistry refers to the hormones and chemicals found inside a living being, influencing their state. If the mother is stressed, the baby receives the exact chemical stress response that flows through the mother's system: mostly cortisol and adrenaline. If the mother is generally relaxed and feels at home inside herself during pregnancy, then the baby will also receive the biochemistry that follows those pleasurable feelings: *endorphins*, our feel-good hormones.

For adult humans, our nervous system field is usually about two to three feet in diameter. Once a baby is born, as a survival strategy, they download the nervous system field of their mother's or primary caregiver's called *limbic imprinting* (3). This is even more true for babies who are breastfed—because they are literally inside the mother's nervous system field for much of their infancy.

Therefore, whatever mom is going through, the baby is also going to go through. If mom's nervous system is healthy, the baby will also imprint a healthy nervous system. If mom has a secure attachment, a deep seat in her authenticity, and knows she belongs, her baby will imprint the positive biochemistry that accompanies this state of health, too. Then with this stable foundation, as babies start growing stronger and more independent and, therefore, need less time in direct contact with mom, they will develop their own nervous system field that is separate from their mother's. This usually begins to happen around age two and a half and also coincides with the time in a healthy child's development when they take an interest in playing with other children. And this is a beautiful and health-full sign.

If mom's nervous system is not healthy, if she has unprocessed trauma, is chronically stressed out and overwhelmed, and has an insecure attachment herself, the baby will inevitably imprint that biochemistry, literally drinking in stress hormones through her breast milk. Even if the baby is not breastfed or if the primary caregiver is not the mother, they will imprint the nervous system field of the individual who is primarily involved in caring for them. The stress held within the household environment can also create insecurity in a child's vulnerable nervous system, challenging attachment, and impacting bonding.

However, even with a stressed biochemistry and challenging environment, children can still stand a chance to develop a secure attachment and that has to do with *attunement*. Let me explain.

Attunement

Babies are wired for survival. Therefore, all interpretations of early life are filtered into two main categories: safety and survival or lack of safety and threat to survival. For an infant, pain elicits a threat response, as does feeling hungry (the window of tolerance for an infant is quite narrow at first). However, things like eye contact, touch, and something called attunement are the primary actions that lead to an infant feeling safe and reducing a threat response. When babies have access to this parasympathetic, rest and digest state regularly, they are more likely to reach developmental milestones and become functional, healthy, balanced adults.

Attunement describes the capacity for a caregiver to be able to read the signs and signals of an infant or someone otherwise dependent on them. If a baby is upset, for instance, a healthy caregiver is going to respond to the baby in an attuned way: sensitively with loving sounds and/or with comforting touch. They will respond with some concern as they are trying to figure out why the baby is upset. And that is a sign of an attuned caregiver.

When a baby is happy, a healthy, attuned caregiver is witnessing this and responding appropriately. Seeing the baby smiling, a healthy caregiver is going to feel the natural impulse to smile back. If the baby has some digestive discomfort and is upset, a healthy and attuned caregiver is going to pick up on this change in the baby's demeanor and respond appropriately with care and concern.

Mirror Neurons and Our Need for Other Humans

Attunement comes out of our unique capacity as mammals to develop *mirror neurons*. Mirror neurons are a type of brain cell found in abundance in all mammals that enable us to recognize and empathize with emotion in other living beings. We have millions of these cells in our brains and they are what both enables us to feel connected *to* and care *for* others as well as what allows us to drink in connection, care, and empathy *from* others.

When you are healthy (i.e., *not* stuck in a trauma response), mirror neurons wire you to see the similarities in other human and nonhuman beings. You can feel others' joy as though it is your own. You can feel others' pain as though it is your own (within reason—good boundaries are essential). When you are healthy, you will *want* to be surrounded by other healthy humans and it will become easy to give and receive compassion, inspiration, and nourishment. This is how we humans are all wired.

However, when trauma happens and you become stuck in a traumatized state, your mirror neuron system goes haywire and this natural desire for human connection (and skill in sustaining it) gets interrupted. The entire social engagement branch of the nervous system may go offline. You may not be able to see yourself in the "other," and, in fact, other humans may become frightening. Simply being around other human beings can lead to high levels of anxiety and fear when there is unhealed trauma. Your boundaries can become discombobulated, and you may not be able to track where you end and others begin. Like cold-blooded animals, you may find yourself living at the mercy of what is happening in your environment. This can be an overwhelming experience and can understandably make it difficult to want to be in any kind of close relationship with other humans.

In family systems, you have family members who have all grown up mirroring each other. In healthy family systems, this is wonderful and leads to healthy, resourced humans, generation after generation. However, in unhealthy family systems where there is unhealed trauma, you have mirror neurons mirroring the trauma responses of the family members and these are the places where unhealed trauma gets passed down through the family lineage.

Mirror neurons teach us about what behavior is welcomed in our society and what isn't. When you behave in a manner that is in alignment with your society's standards, you get to be a part of society and reap the benefits of society (nourishment, guidance, attention, love, safety, protection, etc.). When you behave in a manner that is out of alignment with your society's standards, you will know it because the benefits will begin to retract (people won't want to be near you anymore and your access to benefits may dwindle). This aspect of mammal biology has contributed to our survival instincts and our attachment to other humans and has historically supported us in staying connected to our communities. While our Western society is very different now than it was during hunter-gatherer times, we humans have the same biology and the same needs.

Mirror neurons give us the capacity to attune, and attunement enables us to see the joy or the distress in others, feel empathy, and respond in a way that creates connection and lets the other know, "I see you." Children with well-attuned caregivers become adults who easily attune to friends, family, community members, to pets, and other sentient beings as well. This is largely what creates a secure attachment style, which then creates an adult who is resilient and who knows they belong.

Secure Attachment

Secure attachment styles lead to children and adults who have a significant amount of personal resources that lead to a high self-esteem, emotional intelligence, strong, trusting, long-lasting friendships, romantic relationships, and an unshakeable sense of belonging. With a secure attachment style, you can traverse life's greatest challenges with a wide window of tolerance and higher resilience to stress. This doesn't mean you aren't rocked by life. Rather, you have a secure foundation to call you back home to yourself more quickly and efficiently after experiencing even extreme challenges (remember the tetherball analogy). Secure attachment styles serve as the foundation in human beings who know without a doubt that they belong—in their bodies and on the Earth.

Traits of a Secure Attachment Style

The following are other characteristics of having a secure attachment style. I hope you begin salivating while you read them:

+ You know you belong, you feel valuable and worthy.

+ You, generally, have a positive view of yourself and others.

+ It feels easy and comforting to be emotionally close with others.

+ You feel comfortable leaning on others and having others lean on you.

+ You feel comfortable with distance from others, and it doesn't automatically translate into worry about being alone or not feeling accepted by others.

+ In general, you find others trustworthy and dependable.

+ You exhibit a balance of both intimacy and independence.

+ You are resilient in body, mind, and spirit.

+ You naturally feel your interdependence with the Earth.

+ You source from both your own internal resources as well as external resources.

+ You are able to set boundaries with confidence.

+ You are aware of and care for other sentient beings on the planet.

+ You know who you are and (at least some of) what lives in your shadow.

+ You find it easy to feel compassion for others who are suffering without taking on their suffering as though it is your own. For example: when you can be with another being who is in distress and can feel empathy but you do not feel like you need to be in distress as well.

Sounds amazing, right?

But this isn't why you are here. You are here because you want to learn about what happens when a secure attachment style does not come to fruition. You want to know what has happened to so many of us humans who have not grown up in this way and what you can do about it.

Misattunement and Insecure Attachment

Just as the capacity to attune is a big deal, the experience of *misattunement* is also a big deal. This happens when a parent or caregiver's own capacity to attune to their child is hindered. As a one-off experience, misattunement can be no biggie, especially if a child or adult already has developed some ability to tap into their own resources. However, if this becomes a recurring experience, chronic misattunement can lead to the development of an insecure attachment style or even an experience that becomes traumatizing. Let's explore misattunement further.

If a baby is smiling and looking at mom or the primary caregiver and this behavior elicits a reaction of loving touch, kind words, and eye contact, the baby has now wired into their brain a way to gather feelings of safety from the caregiver and the environment. When this reaction from the primary caregiver is consistent, it will provide a feeling of safety that liberates the baby's attention from survival to play and wonder, enabling them to explore and develop important physical, social, and emotional skills.

If, on the other hand, a baby cries and, in response to the crying, the primary caregiver turns away and does not touch or nurture the baby through sound or loving eye contact, the baby then experiences a threat response. This then takes the baby's attention away from their explorations and puts it back onto the caregiver to better ensure their safety and survival.

A baby in a threat response will produce the same stress hormones as an adult in survival mode and if they are not able to resource (remember, babies resource through contact with their primary caregiver), they can get stuck trying to process energies that are far outside of their window of tolerance. If this experience happens repeatedly, the baby will go into a trauma response, which could look like inconsolable crying, extremely needy behavior, shut down/quiet, complicit, and/or flat or expressionless. These behaviors can be indicative of the fight, flight, freeze, and fawn responses in an infant who has far less capacity for expression than an adult under threat. The child ultimately develops a confusing relationship with their needs—because she has learned that the feeling of having a need has become associated with a threat to her survival.

Babies and children who are experiencing a threat response will try to make sense of why this is happening to them. Their psyches can go in one of two directions: *my caregiver is bad* or *I am bad*. Because, as little ones, we need our caregivers to ensure our survival, most of us develop the *I am bad* paradigm because it is far too scary to think that our caregiver is bad. This single thought can set us up for a lifetime of struggle as it becomes part of our operating system as adults. The *I am bad* paradigm creates shame, isolation, and blocks us from feeling lovable, from feeling our authentic expression, and from sensing our innate belonging. Chronic misattunement in childhood is frequently the root cause of fawning behavior in adults. We have downloaded the messaging that *we are the bad ones*, and we tend to feel safer if we can attune to others and to things happening outside of ourselves rather than attuning to our own bodies and psyches' needs, guidance, and wisdom.

Misattunement in childhood can happen for a number of reasons and is rarely intentional. More often than not, chronic misattunement happens when the parent or caregiver has unhealed trauma living in their own nervous system and is unresourced themselves. Unhealed trauma, as you can see, stunts the development of mirror neurons, literally disabling our capacity for attunement.

Underneath our own unhealed trauma is typically a deep well of unmet need. When you have dissociated from your own needs, you frequently can't see (or can't tolerate) others having those needs either. This challenges your ability to have empathy and express compassion, even with your own children.

And since, as humans, we repeat what we don't repair, sometimes our parents or caregivers are simply repeating what they learned about parenting from how they were parented. If your parents did not have attuned caregivers, and have not done their work to tend to those wounds, then they are less likely to develop attunement with their own children. If you did not have attuned parents, and you have not done your work to tend to those wounds, then you are less likely to attune to your own children; and the generational cycle of chronic misattunement (i.e., trauma) begins. Symptoms of unhealed trauma can lead to a preoccupation for the caregiver and can make attunement even more out of reach.

Attunement in childhood turns out to be the very thing that decides our emotional fate as adults; this includes how you handle stress, how anxious you become, how connected you feel to the world, and how you bond with your loved ones—or not. When you experience frequent misattunement during childhood, you become traumatized and learn to sever from your needs as a coping strategy. You are then likely to develop an insecure attachment style that will challenge your ability to function as a healthy, present, secure adult. You will struggle with a sense of belonging anywhere outside yourself because you don't even feel as though you belong inside your own skin.

Disclaimer: Parenting is not about perfection; ruptures are expected to happen and yet repairing after a rupture is important. Ruptures without repair create the attachment wounds we see today. However, research now shows us that ruptures *with* repair shortly after, create more resilience and stronger relationships than if there was no rupture at all (4). Misattunement is a rupture that does not happen deliberately. Most parents want only the best for their children, but they might not have the resources they need to be able to offer that in the moments that matter. I invite you to hold compassion for yourself if you are a parent and for your own parents and caregivers as you explore this territory with me. We are all only doing the best with what we've got at any given moment, after all. And as adults, we can heal from the trauma of chronic misattunement. More on that in Part Three. For more resources on parenting, see page 235.

Insecure Attachment

Insecure attachment often sits at the core of our personal traumas for those of us who struggle with a sense of not belonging in adulthood and a disconnection from our authentic expression. And this directly results from challenges in our childhood. Insecure attachment wounds can leave us feeling as though no matter what you do, or how far you've come, none of the healing work seems to stick long enough to fill the void of belonging. That's because, with an insecure attachment, that secure base—the stable tetherball pole—isn't there. Instead, you have a rope that hangs in the abyss. All of your actions and feelings might be underpinned with insecurity (the *I am bad* paradigm, remember). Not only will you struggle to find a sense of belonging among other humans, but also in your body and on the Earth. You will too easily feel separate and alone.

Insecure attachment styles lead to low self-esteem, an inability to seek out support when needed (or seeking out support constantly even when not truly needed), unable to lean on others or allow others to lean on you, an inability to establish long-lasting friendships or romantic relationships, and difficulty sharing your true feelings with others for fear that you may displease someone (displeasing someone often awakens a threat response according to the insecure nervous system). But most of all, insecure attachment blocks us from feeling a sense of belonging and holds just out of reach of our innate sense of resilience and authentic expression.

In the 1970s, psychologist Mary Ainsworth further expounded on Bowlby's attachment theory and discovered three distinct types of insecure attachment styles (5), all of which lead to a high degree of anxiety and insecurity in adulthood:

1. Anxious-Preoccupied (also called Anxious-Ambivalent)

2. Avoidant-Dismissive

3. Fearful-Avoidant (also called Disorganized)

Here are some important notes on these insecure attachment styles:

+   Almost all of our anxiety in adulthood can be traced back to our attachment style.

+   Almost all adults with insecure attachment styles struggle with some type of addiction, whether to alcohol and drugs or workaholism and perfectionism. This is an attempt to fill a void—to feel tethered to a secure base.

+   We almost always adopt the attachment style of our primary caregiver but sometimes we develop the style of our other caregiver (who is often—though not always—the opposite attachment style of our primary caregiver).

+   We almost always choose a partner with the opposite attachment style (if you're anxious, you will probably choose someone avoidant, and if you're avoidant, you will probably choose someone anxious. This is called the anxious-avoidant trap, and there are many books and articles written on the subject!).

+   All three insecure attachment styles cause significant anxiety because of the disorientation to health.

+ All three insecure attachment styles cause confusion over boundaries. For those with the anxious-preoccupied style, they mostly present with a lack of boundaries. For those with the avoidant-dismissive style, they mostly present with excessive or rigid boundaries. For those with the fearful-avoidant style, they tend to flip-flop between the two.

+ You can have one insecure attachment style with partners and lovers and a different insecure attachment style with parents or other authority figures.

+ All insecure attachment styles block a person from developing a sense of belonging.

+ Attachment styles are not static; we can shift in and out of different attachment styles when relating with different people in our lives. For example, you could be anxiously attached with your partner but have an avoidant attachment with a parent. We will always, however, have a default attachment style.

Understanding your insecure attachment style is important as it serves as the gateway to understanding personal traumas you carry from your childhood. If you have not worked to discover and heal those early attachment wounds, to heal from the trauma of chronic misattunement, you will continue to express the same ingrained patterns leading to high anxiety and challenges with feeling your own sense of belonging, resilience, and authenticity. Let's explore the three different attachment styles to gain a better understanding of your inner landscape.

Anxious-Preoccupied Attachment

My needs will never be met, is a common mantra for someone with an anxious-preoccupied attachment style. This attachment style forms as a response to a parent who is attuned sometimes but not others. This leads to a child developing high anxiety, not knowing which type of parent they will be receiving each day: the attuned one or the unattuned one. Developing a trauma response, they eventually become hypervigilant, tracking the outside world instead of their own needs and instincts to find safety. This creates a child (and eventually an adult) who becomes preoccupied with others and unable to soothe themselves, which is an important developmental milestone.

When this child grows up, they will have learned to externalize their needs. Instead of sourcing comfort from inside themselves, they will consistently attempt to source it from the outside through.an over-preoccupation with the outside world, with relationships, with material things, with others' opinions of them, with beauty and aesthetics, and so on. They can overly focus on what others think of them, even to the point of adopting others' beliefs about them rather than generating their own feelings of self-worth. This is the ultimate in fawning behavior, which we must remember is a trauma response and not a personality trait.

Those with an anxious attachment style tend to get lost in the service of others. Meeting others' needs becomes a distraction from feeling and meeting their own needs. They frequently learn to sever from their own needs—perhaps even convincing themselves that they, in fact, have no needs. Remember, to feel need when you have an insecure attachment style leads to a threat response in the nervous system. If you think this sounds like you, check the resource list you created in Chapter One—were there any resources you listed that come from inside yourself or were they all externally sourced?

An anxious-preoccupied attachment style can block a person's direct sense of themselves and innate sense of belonging because their capacity to receive guidance from their own inner compass is disabled. Their attachment wounds have made it difficult for them to trust themselves.

Traits of an anxious-preoccupied attachment style include:

+ **Lack of boundaries:** Where do I end and others begin? Can tend to take on other people's stuff without knowing it.

+ **Lack of risk-taking:** Wants to stay in their comfort zone—even small risks can send them into a trauma response.

+ **High anxiety:** Anxiety permeates everything.

+ **Preoccupation with others and what they think of them:** Difficulty getting out of their heads and constantly worried about what others are thinking of them and how they are perceived.

+ **Fear of being alone, feeling abandoned:** Solitude only increases anxiety and leads to feelings of abandonment.

+ **Overly communicative:** Can even create conflict where there is none just to be able to keep a pulse on what is happening for those around her.

Avoidant-Dismissive Attachment

I have no needs, is a common mantra for someone with an avoidant-dismissive attachment style. This attachment style forms as a response to a parent who is unable to attune to the child's emotional needs and might even be dismissive of them. This is where you see distorted interpretations of tough love. A parenting situation like this might put expectations on a baby to develop their own coping strategies long before it's developmentally possible (using the cry-it-out method unskillfully, for example).

This is where the anxious and avoidant attachment style caregivers differ. The parent of the anxious-preoccupied child doesn't allow the child to develop internal coping strategies, but the parent of the avoidant-dismissive child expects the child to develop coping strategies long before they are ready.

In psychology, the trauma of chronic misattunement leads these children to become what is called *pseudo-independent*. These children, though they appear extremely independent, aren't actually independent; they've learned a strategy of disconnecting from their own needs in order to survive. They learned to appease when very young and might even appear to be extremely generous. This is the double-edged sword: these children can be easily mistaken as overly independent, leading to behaviors from caregivers and other adults that continuously reinforce the independence of the child ("they've got this, they're gonna be fine").

Feeling emotions, in general, can be really difficult for an adult who's grown up in this environment. They'll often do everything in their power to never set themselves up to rely on someone for something (hence the avoidant behavior).

Those with an avoidant attachment style can develop an over-preoccupation with themselves and their own thoughts, frequently getting lost in their work, in their studies, and even in spirituality. Connecting with the divine, God, Gaia, etc., becomes a distraction from feeling and meeting their own needs. On the other end of the spectrum, many adults with this attachment style can also become nihilistic (the abyss at the end of the rope, remember?).

This attachment style can block a person's direct sense of themselves and innate sense of belonging because their capacity to receive guidance and care from the world outside of themselves is disabled. Their attachment wounds have made it difficult for them to trust others. This loss of reciprocity acts as a barrier to belonging.

Traits of an avoidant-dismissive attachment style include:

+ **Excessive or rigid boundaries:** Often after a childhood of being at the mercy of the caregivers' needs, boundaries become a way to find sovereignty.

✦ **Overly risk-taking behaviors:** Having developed a high level of skills in self-soothing, this person often feels comfortable stretching into uncharted territory—even into self-injurious behaviors or suicide attempts.

✦ **High anxiety:** Pervasive, although from the outside, this person can seem aloof.

✦ **Preoccupation with others and what they think of them.**

✦ **Fear of being inundated:** Overtaken by other people's energies and their agendas again, often due to parenting, can present as a need for a large amount of personal space.

✦ **Under-communicative, tends to avoid conflict:** Walking away from conflict can often feel less threatening than sticking around to have it. This pattern leads to superficial relationships that don't last long.

Fearful-Avoidant Attachment

The fearful-avoidant attachment style, also referred to as the disorganized attachment style, is a mixture of the other two insecure attachment styles. This attachment style often presents in the nervous system of a child as the result of a parent who has behaviors of mistrust leading to a child who struggles with what we call in psychology, *a double bind*.

A double bind is used to describe a situation when you are presented with two irreconcilable ways of responding or no options that are health promoting. For a child, this could look like having a need and yet the person who would typically meet that need (i.e., your primary caregiver) is unpredictable and untrustworthy. This creates an internal conflict for the child where their only option is to deal with the need going unmet (similar to the way a person with an avoidant-dismissive attachment style learns to self-soothe far too early) or to deal with the consequences of going to a parent who may or may not be available (which creates significant anxiety for the child). Double-binds are tricky and can lead to significant fragmentation of the psyche. Hence the traits of this attachment style swing to both ends of the spectrum (both anxious and avoidant, afraid of both abandonment and inundation).

Most often, this attachment style presents when there is abuse happening inside the home, either directly to the child or from one parent to the other, where the child is aware and even possibly witnesses the abuse. This unpredictable behavior from a person of trust leads to a child who feels confused about how to get their needs met.

In my practice, I have found that many clients who suffer from a fearful-avoidant attachment style are frequently diagnosed with Bipolar Disorder and/or Borderline Personality Disorder. This happens because to be anxious, fearful, and avoidant simultaneously often leads to confusion regarding nourishment: "I am scared and want comfort and assurance from you, but I am also aware that you could turn into the very thing I'm scared of, so I need to be cautious and also protect myself so please stay away." We then see inconsistent behaviors that reflect this very polarity they feel inside.

This attachment style can block a person's access to authentic expression and innate sense of belonging because their capacity to receive guidance and care from inside or outside of themselves is disabled. Their attachment wounds have made it difficult for them to trust both themselves and others. This loss of trust and connection blocks a person from sensing their innate belonging.

Traits of a fearful-avoidant attachment style include:

+ **Sometimes difficulty setting boundaries and other times excessive or rigid boundaries:** Confusion over what is healthy and nourishing is common.

+ **Overly risk-taking behaviors, often impulsive:** Sometimes the confusion over what is healthy and nourishing leads to reacting quickly, without forethought.

+ **High anxiety:** Having experienced such unpredictability in childhood, many people with this attachment style will have extraordinarily high anxiety.

+ **Preoccupation with others and what they think of them:** With a learned distrust in other humans, these adults tend to overanalyze and become hypervigilant about controlling what others think of them.

+ **Fear of being both rejected as well as inundated:** This leads to behaviors that can be confusing, where they both signal others to come close and also to go away and keep their distance.

+ **Sometimes under-communicative and sometimes overly communicative:** Again, this is reflective of the confusion they feel about nourishment.

AS YOU CAN SEE, chronic misattunement in childhood cracks the foundation of our well-being, leading to significant vulnerability and trauma. And without access to resources (or resourced caregivers), children will develop insecure attachment styles. This is precisely how our traumas get carried down through the lineage: whatever attachment wounds remain unresolved will automatically impact those around us through our nervous systems' need to imprint, most especially those who are dependent on us like our children. This also explains why—try as we might to be nothing like our caregivers—we end up so much like them. But it is also this early wounding that sets us up for the vulnerable psychology we have as adults (and many of our strengths, too, but more on that later).

The most important thing to note about insecure attachment styles, in addition to understanding and developing compassion for how they can impact *literally every aspect of your life*, is that they can be healed. Insecure attachment does not heal on its own; rather, it takes effort, strategy, and resources. There is an encouraging body of research in psychology revealing that we humans are able to repair from an insecure attachment style and when we do this, it is called *earned secure attachment.* Earned secure attachment is a phrase developed by John Bowlby, years after his discovery of attachment (2). It is used to describe the journey of repairing from what was missing in childhood to essentially re-parent yourself into a healthier, more resilient adulthood. He suggests we can do this by developing a relationship with another healthy human who can—over time and with strategy, provide our nervous systems with an opportunity to experience the benefits of a secure attachment. More on this in Part Three.

It feels important to mention that attachment is not the single deciding factor in whether we will become more vulnerable to trauma and struggle with our sense of belonging. I have known plenty of people who have had a secure attachment and have struggled in many other ways. Vice versa, I have also known many people who have an insecure attachment style, and yet they feel a strong sense of belonging to their bodies, their communities, and to the Earth. Attachment is an important factor when it comes to physical, spiritual, and emotional health; however, there are many other factors to consider, such as those listed in the Risk and Resiliency section in Chapter Two.

AN INVITATION:
Identifying Your Attachment Style

The first step toward understanding how attachment has impacted you and your family is to take an attachment style quiz. The following is a questionnaire designed to measure your attachment, and it is based on the Experience in Close Relationships (ECR) questionnaire first published in 1998 by Kelly Brennan, Catherine Clark, and Phillip Shaver. This version has been modified by Dr. Amir Levine and Rachel S.F. Heller, MA, in their book *Attached: Are you Anxious, Avoidant or Secure? How the Science of Adult Attachment Can Help You Find—and Keep—Love* published in 2010. If you would prefer to take a fully validated online version, visit: http://www.web-research-design. net/cgi-bin/crq/crq.pl. If you register for the online version and select Option A, you can log in periodically on your healing journey, retake the quiz, and watch your attachment style change.

Check the small box next to each statement that is true for you. If the answer is untrue for you, do not check the box or mark the column at all.

Attachment Style Quiz	True		
	A	B	C
I often worry that my partner will stop loving me.			
I find it easy to be affectionate with my partner.			
I fear that once someone gets to know the real me, they won't like who I am.			
I find that I bounce back quickly after a breakup. It's weird how I can just put someone out of my mind.			
When I'm not involved in a relationship, I feel somewhat anxious and incomplete.			
I find it difficult to emotionally support my partner when they are feeling down.			
When my partner is away, I'm afraid that they might become interested in someone else.			
I feel comfortable depending on romantic partners.			
My independence is more important to me that my relationships.			
I prefer not to share my innermost feelings with my partner.			
When I show my partner how I feel, I'm afraid they will not feel the same about me.			
I am generally satisfied with my romantic relationships.			
I don't feel the need to act out much in my romantic relationships.			
I think about my relationships a lot.			
I find it difficult to depend on romantic partners.			
I tend to get very quickly attached to a romantic partner.			
I have little difficulty expressing my needs and wants to my partner.			

Attachment Style Quiz	True		
	A	B	C
I sometimes feel angry or annoyed with my partner without knowing why.			
I am very sensitive to my partner's moods.			
I believe most people are essentially honest and dependable.			
I prefer casual sex with uncommitted partners to intimate sex with one person.			
I'm comfortable sharing my personal thoughts and feelings with my partner.			
I worry if my partner leaves me I might never find someone else.			
It makes me nervous when my partner gets too close.			
During a conflict, I tend to impulsively do or say things I later regret, rather than be able to reason about things.			
An argument with my partner doesn't usually cause me to question our entire relationship.			
My partners often want me to be more intimate than I feel comfortable being.			
I worry that I'm not attractive enough.			
Sometimes people see me as boring because I create little drama in relationships.			
I miss my partner when we're apart, but then when we're together I feel the need to escape.			
When I disagree with someone, I feel comfortable expressing my opinions.			
I hate feeling that other people depend on me.			
If I notice that someone I'm interested in is checking out other people, I don't let it faze me. I might feel a pang of jealousy, but it's fleeting.			
I have little difficulty expressing my needs and wants to my partner.			

Attachment Style Quiz			
	True		
	A	B	C
If I notice that someone I'm interested in is checking out other people, I feel relieved—it means they are not looking to make things exclusive.			
If I notice that someone I'm interested in is checking out other people, it makes me feel depressed.			
If someone I've been dating begins to act cold and distant, I may wonder what's happened, but I'll know it's probably not about me.			
If someone I've been dating begins to act cold and distant, I'll probably be indifferent; I might even be relieved.			
If someone I've been dating begins to act cold and distant, I'll worry that I've done something wrong.			
If my partner was to break up with me, I'd try my best to show them what they are missing (a little jealously can't hurt).			
If someone I've been dating for several months tells me they want to stop seeing me, I'd feel hurt at first, but I'd get over it.			
Sometimes when I get what I want in a relationship, I'm not sure what I want anymore.			
I won't have much of a problem staying in touch with my ex (strictly platonic)—after all, we have a lot in common.			

Adapted from Fraley, Waller and Brennan's (2000) ECR-R Questionnaire.

Add up all your checked boxes in Column A: _____

Add up all your checked boxes in Column B:_____

Add up all your checked boxes in Column C:_____

Scoring Key

The more statements you checked in a category will represent the more characteristics you display in the corresponding attachment style. Category A represents the *anxious* attachment style. Category B represents the *secure* attachment style, and Category C represents the *avoidant* attachment style. If you have an equal number of checked boxes between Category A and C, it is possible you have a fearful-avoidant attachment style.

Now that you have identified your primary attachment style, if you discovered it is an insecure attachment style, take a few deep breaths. Remember, these did not develop because *you are bad,* these developed because you have a strong will to survive, and this is what you had to do to ensure your survival. Give yourself a squeeze. Perhaps take a moment and engage in another practice from Part One. You are doing amazing. And if something has awakened in you through this quiz and you feel the need to seek professional support, please pause and take care of yourself. There are many trauma-informed and compassionate practitioners who have the capacity and the skills to see you through this time.

Healing from attachment wounds can (and should) also include working with your biochemistry. If you have identified yourself as having an insecure attachment style, not only has your psychology been impacted, but your biochemical processes have also been impacted, too. So while you want to work at the level of your psychology, you also want to work at the level of your body's accompanying chemistry. And there are a number of ways to work with this through nutrition, herbal medicine, supplementation, lifestyle adjustments, practices, and lab testing. Please see my first book, *Everyday Chinese Medicine: Healing Remedies for Immunity, Vitality, and Optimal Health,* for a more complete guide in healing the biochemical aspect of the stress and trauma responses.

CHAPTER SIX:
ANCESTRAL TRAUMA

AS YOU CAN SEE, unhealed trauma can be carried from one generation to the next through our attachment styles. What this means is that *we didn't come into our families as blank slates.* Each generation is undoubtedly influenced by the generation that came before because of our need to survive as infants and consequential imprinting on members in our family and in the environment in which we were raised.

Therefore, any unhealed trauma in your family's lineage can be brought through many generational lines and land in your family system, even from ancestors who you had no direct physical contact with.

Most trauma gets passed down ancestrally because of the patterns found in your *family system.* The family system is a term used to describe the family unit as an organism. It was a theory developed in the 1950s by psychiatrist Murray Bowen (1), where he discovered that there is an "emotional system governing human relationships within families." In each family system there are specific roles and rules that are sometimes implicit and other times explicit. I believe this explains why in certain families, patterns, and behaviors of unhealed trauma can become passed down in such a way that we don't even see that we have taken them on, and yet they are given the power to govern our lives.

I have worked with many clients who are experiencing trauma responses in their current lives and yet they, themselves do not identify as someone who has experienced trauma.

This generational transference of unhealed trauma is called *transgenerational trauma*. Transgenerational trauma was first acknowledged by the American Psychological Association when conducting studies with Nazi concentration camp survivors. What they discovered is that the children of survivors often also displayed symptoms of *Post-Traumatic Stress Disorder (PTSD)* even though they themselves were never exposed to the stress and horrors of the concentration camps (2).

PTSD is a psychological disorder typically diagnosed after a traumatic experience or the witnessing of a traumatic experience when a person does not easily return to their healthy, pre-trauma state of functioning. Flashbacks, nightmares, severe anxiety, and even constantly reliving the trauma in a person's mind or body are the key symptoms leading to this diagnosis. For young children, PTSD can often look like nightmares, bed-wetting, regression in speaking, being suddenly and extremely clingy, and even reenacting the traumatic event through play or art.

For symptoms as life-altering as these, this speaks to the power of trauma and the nervous system field and why it is important to learn what kind of family system you came from so you can better understand what you carried into this life with you.

It's important to note that transgenerational trauma is also what leads to *cycles of violence* within family systems and communities. Cycles of violence are when we see children mimicking the unhealed trauma responses of their caregivers, and the parents mimicking the unhealed trauma responses of their caregivers, and so on. This happens because a child's nervous system imprints on the parent's nervous system (as a survival strategy), and it doesn't matter to the child if it is a healthy nervous system or not. All that matters is survival.

All the unhealed trauma in your family system now lives inside of you and is expressed through your nervous system. How you have learned to operate in the world, even though it may feel like you are in the driver's seat, has been heavily influenced by your ancestors and their experiences. If you don't know what kind of family system you come from, then it is difficult to know what you carry with you; not only your challenges, but your strengths, too. The stories we inherited from our ancestors are revealed through our relationship to health, our relationship to scarcity, to power, to feelings of separateness or belonging, and so on. These are subconscious downloads that come through the lineage. To be clear, your ancestors' wounds are not *your* wounds. However, the consequences of them can become part of your wounding. Attachment wounds are a perfect example of this.

Not surprisingly, it is this very capacity we humans encompass to mirror and imprint on each other that also makes transgenerational healing possible. More on this later.

Epigenetic Trauma

Attachment styles aren't the only way that trauma gets passed down through a lineage. Another way is through *epigenetics*. Epigenetics, an ever-expanding field we could write an entire book on, but simply put, explains the role that chronic stress and trauma play in our human growth and development. Epigenetics differs from genetics in that genetics have to do with what is encoded in a particular gene. For example, the genetic DNA for an oak tree informs that the tree will produce oak-like leaves, acorns, and grow to be similar to other oak trees. However, the epigenetics of the oak tree acts more like an instruction manual for the oak's DNA and is impacted by its age, its behavior (mostly related to animated beings), and the environment.

Suppose an oak tree was constantly being trimmed, mutilated, and otherwise stressed in its environment. The seeds produced by that oak tree are going to be impacted by this stress, leading to potentially strange oak tree characteristics once they germinate and grow, such as: developing a smaller stature, growing fewer limbs, growing in directions other than toward the sun, and so on. This is the *epigenetic expression influencing the genetics* of an oak tree.

We, humans, are no different. Chronic stress and trauma in our environment and in the environment of our parents and grandparents can cause us to experience a form of trauma that gets passed down through the family line, influencing our nervous system, our attachment, and our psyche. We may have no recollection of a trauma. However, we may exhibit trauma response behaviors like the oak that was no longer expressing typical characteristics of an oak tree.

The important thing to remember with epigenetics is that unlike genetics, they are workable and reversible. If a person has a genetic mutation, we can't take that mutated gene away from them. However, we can do everything we can to try to keep it turned off by reducing stress and other risk factors as well as increasing resiliency through building resources.

Given this, I hope you can understand why I find it important to know as much as you are able to about what kind of family system you come from. Not only who raised you but also how, what the environment was like, what the culture was like, what stressors your family faced, their beliefs, their unhealed trauma, and more. Knowing where you come from can give you some sense of what you carry with you into this life through your nervous system and epigenetically.

Weaving through the Past

The nervous systems of our ancestors that have the most impact on our individual nervous systems are those of our parents, grandparents, and great-grandparents. Think about it like this: you lived inside of your grandmother as an egg in her ovaries when she was developing in utero inside your great-grandmother. Anything your grandmother went through while she was pregnant with your mom directly impacted you. When your grandmother was an egg inside of her mother, and her mother was growing inside her grandmother's womb, she was being impacted directly by her grandmother's life. And the cycle goes on all the way back to our earliest ancestors.

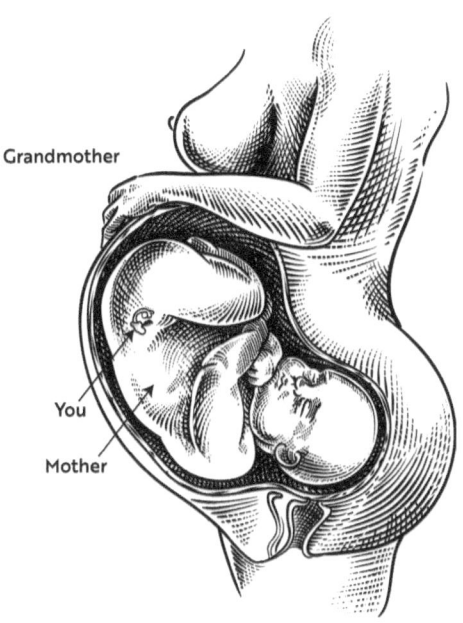

Because of this deep connection you have with your ancestors, your healing journey directly benefits and works to tend to the unhealed trauma carried in your lineage, especially the maternal line. If you carried unhealed trauma with you into this world via your ancestors when you were born and did nothing about it but live a challenging life with little to no access to resources and, therefore, little to no access to healing, you will continue to carry forward this very nervous system field onto those around you—most especially if you have children or little ones who are dependent on you.

However, if you are able to resource yourself during your lifetime and gain access to healing people and healing modalities, you have the opportunity to heal not only your own nervous system, but also influence all the other nervous systems around you. The people around you will be impacted by the healthier vibrations carried in your nervous system and most certainly if you raise children or rescue animals. Children will undoubtedly benefit from your healing work as they can imprint on your healthy nervous system. When this happens, the trauma in a lineage has the opportunity to transform and heal.

Learning about your ancestors is a privilege. Even having the space in your psyche and heart to have this inquiry is a privilege (as it is a sign that you are not—at present—in survival mode). And much of the ancestry data available to us in the Western world is reflective of European ancestors. If you are a person of color, I'm sure you have already noticed how difficult it is to find out about your ancestors. There are some resources available to you on page X if you have difficulty finding out about your family's history.

AN INVITATION:
Create a Psychological Family Tree

Unlike a traditional family tree, a *genogram* is a psychological family tree. With this, you only gather data from a few generations back—usually only great-grandparents or (at the most) great-great-grandparents to see what ancestral trauma may have the most impact on you today.

The important aspect of a genogram is that it helps you see patterns of relationships, addiction, abuse, suicide, mental health challenges, miscarriages, and cycles of violence getting passed down from generation to generation. When you have this visual representation of your psychological family history, you can draw lines through lineages where you can *literally* see the trauma getting passed down from one generation to the next. It can be both frightening and enlightening. You may take your first breath of fresh air once you can see how some of your challenges are actually the wounds of your ancestors that went unhealed.

Of course, when you look back into anyone's family lineage, you will find so much suffering. Allow this information to bring compassion, awareness, and to help you better understand how you got here. Creating a genogram is a remarkable practice to do and one that should be done with consciousness, tenderness, and with personal and ancestral healing in mind.

Unlike a family tree, a genogram is often not shared with anyone else in your family. The reason for this has to do with the personal assessments you will make of your family members. For example, you may label your mother an addict, though she may not see herself that way. You may make note of domestic violence happening between partners. However, the partners may view their squabbles as normal. But remember, this is *your* process of understanding how your nervous system was influenced by those in your family. I find it is more important to be honest in your assessment rather than hold back so as not to hurt others' feelings.

One of the best ways to begin working on your genogram is to take stock of all the family members who are still alive and start asking them about who they remember in their family and what they remember about each person. You will be looking for qualities and patterns in stories. I would start with the oldest family members first and work your way to the youngest. It is truly a blessing to be able to gather all this information. I know so many who—by the time they were interested in this information, had already lost the family members who would have offered significant stories and perspective.

Once you gather your data, ask yourself: what are the themes you have noticed in hearing these stories and in knowing what you know about these family members?

List your themes out. Here are some of the negative themes I would recommend tracking: addiction, suicide, perfectionism, isolation, depression, miscarriages, abortions, alcoholism, workaholism, racist, sexist, LGBTQIA/homophobic, trans/transphobic, abusive (physically and/or verbally), abused, volatile, disconnected (when family member disconnects from contact with other family members), immigrant, and any other patterns you may notice.

Of note: typically, we only track the negative qualities or characteristics in our genograms, but I want to invite you to track some of the positive qualities as well and to include them in your genogram. Here are some of the positive or more neutral themes that I would recommend tracking: sexuality, gender identity, pets, education, language fluency, career choices, relationship status, health status, etc. Gather these themes along with a poster board and colored pencils, and let's put together your genogram.

1. **Start by drawing a shape of your choosing at the bottom center of the paper;** this shape will represent you. Some ideas for shapes are circle, square, star, triangle, rectangle, etc. You could select one shape

to represent the feminine, one shape to represent the masculine, and one shape to represent the non-binary people in your family. Or you could choose one shape per generation. This is your genogram so follow your heart, get creative, and do what makes the most sense to you.

2. **Draw your siblings.** If you have siblings, draw shapes to the left and/ or right of your shape and connect them to your shape using horizontal lines.

3. **Draw your parents.** Then, draw the shapes to represent each of your parents, just above and off center from your shape. Following a typical family tree pattern, draw two lines coming from your shape and connecting to each of your parents.

4. **Draw your grandparents.** Draw four shapes to represent each of your grandparents, just above and off center from your parents' shapes. Draw four lines coming from your parent's shapes connecting to each of your grandparents.

5. **Draw your great-grandparents.** Draw eight shapes to represent each of your great-grandparents, just above and off center from your grandparents' shapes. Draw eight lines coming from your grandparent's shapes connecting to each of your great-grandparents.

6. **Using your themes, create your key.** In one corner of your poster board, add a key. I have included an example of a genogram key here that you can use as you craft your genogram. If you do not find the themes in your own family represented in this key, feel free to add your own. For example, you may decide to add race, religion, ethnicity, and other things to your genogram.

7. **Add psychological information.** Once you have placed your key on your board, add the psychological information into your family's genogram. Use the key to show the relationships between people in your family as well as their individual challenges.

Here is an example of a genogram:

Genogram Template

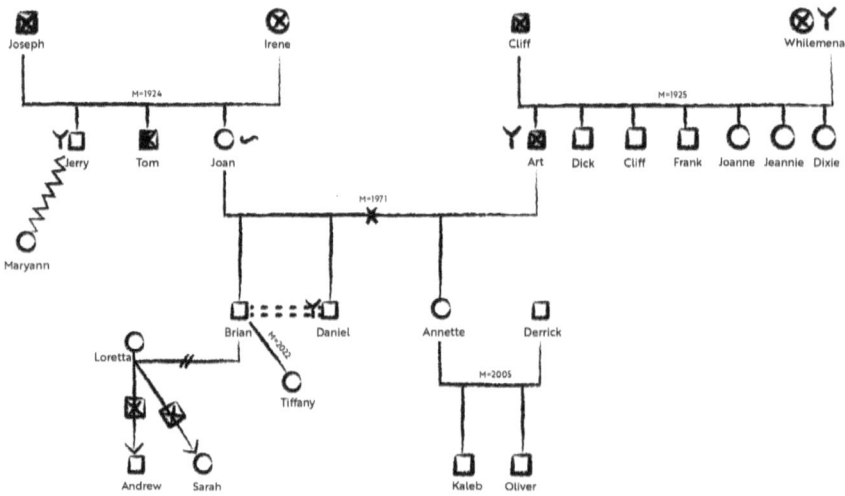

Genogram Key

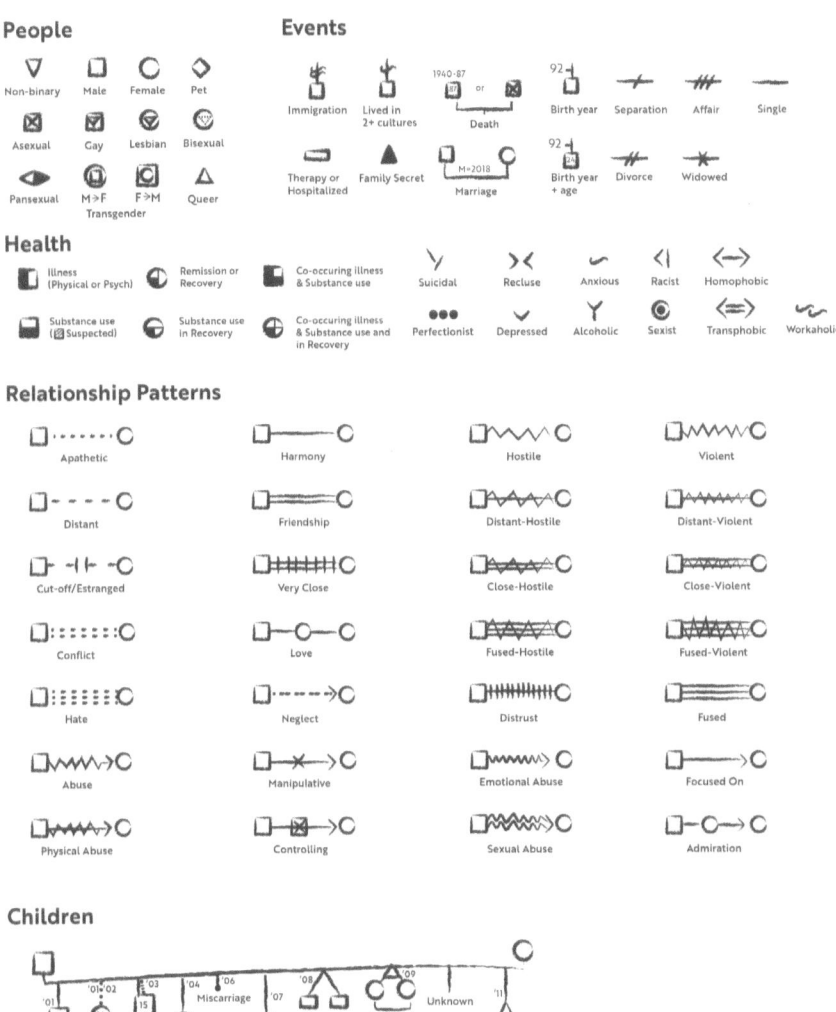

People

▽	☐	○	◇
Non-binary	Male	Female	Pet

Asexual ⊠ · Gay ☑ · Lesbian ⊘ · Bisexual ◉

Pansexual ◈ · M→F 🔵 · F→M 🟥 · Queer △
Transgender

Events

Immigration · Lived in 2+ cultures · 1940-87 or ⊠ Death · Birth year · Separation · Affair · Single

Therapy or Hospitalized · ▲ Family Secret · M→2018 Marriage · 92 Birth year + age · Divorce · Widowed

Health

| Illness (Physical or Psych) | Remission or Recovery | Co-occuring illness & Substance use | ⌄ Suicidal | ✕ Recluse | ↶ Anxious | ⟨∣ Racist | ⟨—⟩ Homophobic |

| Substance use (⊠ Suspected) | Substance use in Recovery | Co-occuring illness & Substance use and in Recovery | ●●● Perfectionist | ⌄ Depressed | ⅄ Alcoholic | ◉ Sexist | ⟨⇔⟩ Transphobic | ∿ Workaholic |

Relationship Patterns

☐·······○ Apathetic	☐——○ Harmony	☐〰〰○ Hostile	☐〰〰○ Violent
☐- - - -○ Distant	☐══○ Friendship	☐▲▲▲○ Distant-Hostile	☐▲▲▲○ Distant-Violent
☐⊣∣⊦○ Cut-off/Estranged	☐╫╫╫○ Very Close	☐▲▲▲○ Close-Hostile	☐▲▲▲○ Close-Violent
☐::::::○ Conflict	☐—○—○ Love	☐▲▲▲○ Fused-Hostile	☐▲▲▲○ Fused-Violent
☐:::::○ Hate	☐·---→○ Neglect	☐╫╫╫○ Distrust	☐══○ Fused
☐〰〰→○ Abuse	☐—✕→○ Manipulative	☐〰〰⟩○ Emotional Abuse	☐——→○ Focused On
☐〰〰→○ Physical Abuse	☐—⊠→○ Controlling	☐〰〰⟩○ Sexual Abuse	☐—○—→○ Admiration

Children

'01'02 · '03 · '04 · '06 Miscarriage · '07 · '08 Identical Twins · '09 · Unknown · '11 Pregnancy

'01 '17 · '16 · Adopted · ⊗ Stillbirth · ✕ Abortion · Twins · Identical Twins
Bio-Child · Foster

Now that you are seeing all of this psychological information about your family in one place, what do you notice? In particular, are there any themes that you see running in your family? Are there patterns that continue from one generation to the next? What can you gather from the psychology of your family members and how it impacted your family system? Do you have at least one healthy ancestor who you can identify and keep your memory of them (or others' memories of them) close?

Of note: Unlike a family tree, a genogram can be crafted without biology in mind. Therefore, people who identify as Black, Indigenous, and/or as a Person of Color (BIPOC) or have been adopted may not have access to the same resources as others, and that's okay in this case. We are tracking the nervous systems that most closely influenced you in your childhood, as well as the ones that most closely influenced the nervous systems of *their* caregivers, and so on.

No matter who you are or what resources you have to dive into this territory, take your time. What you gather in this process can be a lot to digest at once, although it will serve you for life by supporting your understanding of what you unconsciously carried into this life with you through your familial imprinting. Everything you learn in this process will continue to ground you and bring more clarity on your healing journey.

AN INVITATION:
Uncovering Ancestral Wounds

Uncovering wounds that have been passed down through your lineage is a direct way to get to know the psychological framework and the nervous system patterning you may have—even as a survival strategy, unconsciously downloaded. By identifying these wounds and pinpointing a potential source, we begin our work of tending to our ancestral trauma.

Family trees can be amazing sources of information about some of the bigger-picture challenges that have been carried through your family lineage and held in the collective field of your family home and land. The tree allows you to see the journey of your ancestors, where they came from, and the type of emotional and physical environment they were born. I recommend starting to explore here if you don't already have any of this information. You will want to learn not only about where your family originated from but also about the big moments in your culture's history: wars, famines, religious and political views, migrations, and so on that may have impacted you and your family.

Once you have gathered some of this information, here are a few questions for reflection:

+ Who colonized your ancestors, and who did your ancestors colonize?

+ What were their spiritual or religious beliefs?

+ How did they feel about others who did not adopt those beliefs?

✦ Were there battles or wars, plagues, or famines that impacted your family?

✦ Did your family have financial resources or were they poor?

✦ How did they feel about white people, Indigenous people, or people of color?

✦ Who did they see as outsiders?

✦ Who did they see as threats?

✦ Were your ancestors enslaved? Or did they enslave others?

✦ Was your family forced to move and leave behind their homeland?

✦ What was it like for them in their new home? Were they welcome? Or were they shunned?

✦ In other words, what kinds of traumas befell your ancestors and their community?

Answering some or all of these questions can give you a starting place for looking at ancestral trauma that may be impacting you today. Write down all that you learn about your family so that the generations that come after you can have access to this vital information. The more you can know about where you come from, the more you can understand what you carry around with you in your psyche and in your nervous system field. Keep breathing with the plants as you go through this process as it can be tender and bring our awareness to painful aspects of our family history.

Of note: If you are a person who identifies as BIPOC, gathering information about your ancestry may be quite challenging. Sadly, much of the ancestry research found in the West has been focused on European ancestry. There are, however, a few resources for you, and I will put them in the resources section of this book. I hope these resources continue to grow for the BIPOC community.

If you are someone who has been adopted and has no contact with your biological relatives, crafting your family tree might be next to impossible. One way around that is to do an ancestry DNA test to get the locations of where your ancestors were from and research the culture and history of those communities. Resources for this can be found on page 234.

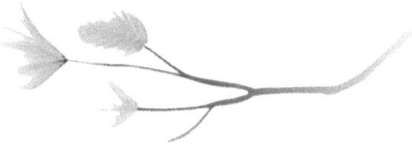

CHAPTER SEVEN:

COLLECTIVE TRAUMA

JUST LIKE THE FAMILY has an emotional system governing the human relationships within it, the culture also has an emotional system governing the human relationships within its communities. Culture is not only made up of the people and practices of a particular location on Earth, but also the elemental energy, plant, animal, and human ancestors, and the energy and stories of the land itself that creates the culture. The cultural system creates what is called a *collective field*, or the *collective* for short. By *collective,* I am referring to the collective of humanity, the collective of your family, your neighborhood, your community, your city, and even your country. It also includes collective groups that you may identify with, such as groups based on gender, ethnicity, religious beliefs, and so on.

The collective holds within it a palpable field of energy. Have you ever walked on to a piece of land, into a town, or into someone's home and immediately felt a shift in energy? This happens because a particular kind of energy is created in response to the history of a place, and the energy of that history is contained in the land, in the structures, and in the nervous systems of the people who live in proximity to it. Think about places like Auschwitz and Hiroshima, these are places that almost immediately stir emotion when you visit them. Living in the foothills of the Rocky Mountains in Ute, Arapaho, and Cheyenne territory, I can feel these energetic shifts constantly, especially as I walk in the mountains or drive through undeveloped areas. It's important to pay attention to these shifts because they are happening around us all the time and we can't help but to be influenced by them, whether we are aware or not.

Trauma can impact us not only personally or ancestrally, but it can also impact us through the energy held in the collective. Trauma in the collective field can be like a forest fire: even though you may not be directly getting burned, the smoke and ash can engulf you. If a community experiences trauma, it is often felt both collectively and personally. As humans, we are undoubtedly impacted by the collective field we exist in.

I find it important to make the distinction between personal, ancestral, and collective trauma because we can sometimes take on ancestral or collective burdens as if they are personal. In fact, I would venture to say that most of us are guilty of this at times. This confusion can lead to a lifetime of struggle and shame because, try as we might, we alone cannot heal collective wounding. If we are able to tease out which of our seemingly personal battles are actually collective, often we find a sense of freedom, relief, camaraderie, and hope.

For example, suppose that you are struggling with chronic anxiety. If something bad happened to you as a child, such as an experience of abuse or neglect from a caregiver, this anxiety could be an example of personal trauma. However, suppose that in your research, you discovered that one or several of your ancestors suffered from extreme hardship such as rape, war, slavery, or famine, then your experience of anxiety might, in fact, be repercussions from the unprocessed traumas of your ancestors.

Or perhaps, you discovered that the very land you call home was once the territory of an Indigenous community that was wiped out through genocide. Your experience of anxiety could very well result from unhealed trauma being held in the collective of the land you are living on. In the first case, doing your personal healing work may soothe your anxiety and give you access to tools for use in moments of intense emotional experiences. In the second case, you may need to do some deeper work, including working with your own ancestors to explore and address the fears that lie underneath and perpetuate your experience of anxiety. In the latter case, talk therapy alone is insufficient at reducing anxiety from collective trauma. When it comes to healing collective trauma, you must—at some point, engage the larger community.

My client, Angela, is a perfect example of someone who was able to track her anxiety to that of collective trauma. In 2010, Angela, who is BIPOC and queer, moved with her partner to Mobile, Alabama, in the occupied and unceded territory of the Choctaw. She had been living in San Francisco, in the occupied and unceded territory of the Ohlone, for most of her adult life but felt ready for a change and was inspired to take a ninth-grade teaching position. After only two months, Angela was struggling with intense feelings of anxiety, bordering on panic—these feelings were foreign to her. She wasn't sleeping well. Her mind was racing when it was time for bed. She felt vulnerable and worried constantly about bad things happening to her and her family even though there was nothing tangible for her to identify as the source. She noticed that the daily short bike ride through town and to her school had become a trigger for her anxiety. She couldn't help but to feel like everyone was watching her when she left her house each morning and came home each evening.

When Angela reached out to me to see about working together virtually to try to resolve this anxiety, she was wondering if the anxiety was from a change in her hormones since she had just turned thirty. As we got to know each other over the course of a few long-distance sessions, I wasn't noticing any other patterns of hormonal imbalance. In fact, a lab test confirmed her hormones were quite balanced for a 30-year old woman. So instead of continuing to dig into her personal experiences and medical history, my intuition told me that Angela needed to find out more about the home she had recently purchased with her partner and the part of town—along with the community she was now living and working in.

In her research, Angela discovered that the land she was living and work-ing on was once home to the Choctaw people. After many years of genocide and forced removal, the land—colonized and occupied by Europeans, became productive farmland due to the use and abuse of slaves from Africa. She also discovered that her neighborhood was only a few miles from a burial ground, where they estimated over 20,000 Choctaw people were murdered and buried. Knowing this history, it quickly became clear that what Angela was experiencing was not likely the result of personal mental health challenges—it was the result of trauma being held in the collective field that her nervous system was picking up on.

Once Angela was able to draw connections between the history of the land, her personal felt experience, and the experiences of other members in her community, she began to feel less anxious, less alone, and more grounded. She began to look into the eyes of those near her and instead of feeling threat-ened, she felt more compassion and curiosity. As a person with the back-ground of a teacher but the heart of a community organizer, Angela decided she wanted to find a way to work within some of the local BIPOC and/or Indigenous Choctaw communities. She applied for and was accepted into a position as a volunteer art teacher for an inner city youth BIPOC after-school art program. This new role fed her spirit so much so that the following year, the nonprofit brought her on as a full-time employee to not only teach art to their BIPOC students, but to also facilitate the creation of new community outreach programs that connected young BIPOC students to elder BIPOC community members through art (and eventually music, storytelling, and food, too!). Her ability to work directly with local, young people of color became the perfect antidote for the nervous system dysregu-lation she experienced from the trauma held in the collective field.

Many collective wounds are buried deep in our psyches and nervous systems, so much so that we might not even know they are there. They can be carried in disguise by the people who live within their field and transmitted through the subliminal messaging of our culture and family lineage. These messages are often downloaded before we have any conscious say in the matter. Without being able to pinpoint the source of our collective wounding, we are fully at its mercy.

One example of collective trauma is the impact of colonization. Whether your ancestors were colonizers, the ones colonized, or both, each generation has had to manage the repercussions of this trauma within their own family systems and collective trauma responses are the same as any trauma responses.

Collective trauma often flies under our radar, and yet it can greatly impact our psyches and experiences. For many of us on both sides of the colonization tracks, I believe a particular collective trauma survival strategy is to write off or ignore our histories. It's true, you might find things in your history that bring up significant shame, fear, or even rage. Yet, the closer you get to understanding what *really* happened—the better you can understand the collective trauma that has impacted you and that you no doubt carry in your nervous system field. This understanding allows you to develop compassion for the ways in which you and your ancestors have learned to operate in the world that perhaps have not been the most conscious or responsible.

For example, many of us non-natives don't realize that we are actually not from this land, this North American continent. It is not common knowledge that we white-bodied folks are in fact, the immigrants in North America. It is not entirely our fault that we don't know this information as much of what we were taught in grade school and in our childhood was the sum of what our teachers and parents were taught. And they didn't know either. Historically, the curriculums in our public school systems have been European-centered and therefore taught only the stories from a colonizer's perspective: the Natives were barbarians and actually *needed* Europeans to save them, among other lies. Most certainly, this was the history that I was taught in grade school.

But feel into this with me for a second: even though you may not consciously know the history of your ancestors and their role in colonization, the very land you are standing on is land that was stolen from Native communities. And given the sensitivity of the human nervous system and the impact of the collective field, is it any wonder that so many of us non-Indigenous people struggle with belonging? As Americans, we have significant work to do to unpack the repercussions of colonization both for ourselves and also for the communities we colonized.

Other examples of collective trauma are the enslavement of people of color, the bombings of Hiroshima and Nagasaki, the attack on Pearl Harbor, terrorist attacks, the COVID-19 pandemic, and even the impossible standards set by the culture we live in, such as beauty, weight, body shape, and size. Additionally, racism, sexism, ageism, ableism, classism, fatism, homophobia, transphobia, xenophobia, religious prejudice, and other forms of oppression can also create a collective field of trauma. More often than not, we grow up in a community that holds one or more of these forms of oppression in its collective field and while we are inevitably impacted by the oppression of it, we might not have the awareness or education to be able to pinpoint where exactly it is coming from.

Another collective field that we are in and are co-creating (if we are participating) is that of social media. Whatever community we form on these platforms will have its own collective fields, some of which can be extremely traumatizing (which is why I think there has been such a mass exodus from social media as of late). And yet, after tragedy, many people have reported finding community and support on social media. We can use these platforms to create something more positive if we are fully aware of what we are participating in and have good boundaries with them.

It is important to mention that not all collective fields are painful and traumatic—they can also be full of positivity. Think about the last time you were witnessing something spectacular at the same time as others, like a full moon eclipse or attending a concert or one of the women's marches. Election days can feel like this, too (especially when the candidate you voted for wins). The joy and feeling of possibility are not only personal—they are collective. And if you are privileged enough, you can even choose positive collective fields that you want to stay within, like choosing to live within a particular community or on specific places on Earth.

AN INVITATION:
Exploring Collective Wounds

Not only is your family history and any intergenerational wounding important to uncover, you will also want to take a look at the history of the land where you are living or where you have spent significant time living to examine the possibility of collective wounds. Land carries so much of the energy of its history within it. And as contagious as collective fields are, you have undoubtedly been impacted by the land in which you call home. The physical home that you occupy is also worth exploring especially if you live in a historic home or in a home that had residents before you. Here are a few questions to answer as you explore this terrain:

+ Where are you living now and where have you spent the bulk of your life living (if it is different than where you are currently living)?

+ How has this landscape changed in the last 5, 10, 50, 100 years?

+ What kind of history does the land you are living on carry with it?

+ Who lived on the land before you?

+ Historically, what was the traditional culture of this land?

+ Was the land stolen from Indigenous people? And if so, who stole it and how?

✦ Were there battles or wars fought on this land?

✦ Were there lynchings on this land?

✦ Who occupied your home before you?

✦ Were there any traumas that you know of that happened in your home before you occupied it?

✦ Are there are burial grounds, cemeteries, historic sites, or national monuments near your home?

Answering some or all of these questions can give you a starting place for looking at collective traumas held in the land that may be impacting you and the people (and even the plants and animals) in your community. Write down all that you learn about the land you call home so that the generations that come after you can have access to this vital information.

If you are a Westerner like me and your ancestors were colonizers, we have significant work to do in this arena. As a starting point, become as educated as you are able regarding the land you are occupying. If you don't already know, take a look at the Native land acknowledgment map featured in the resources section. To take your work a step further, look for organizations that support the Native communities whose land you are occupying and consider making an annual donation to their organization and if welcomed, getting involved in supportive actions that celebrate, honor and sustain their rich culture and community. The more we can understand about our role and our ancestors' roles in these collective fields, the more power we have to work toward healing from trauma—not only personally, collectively also. And in our healing, we release ourselves and our ancestors from the unhealed traumas of the past so that we can move forward with courage and responsibility. As Reverend Angel Kyodo Williams says, "Love and justice are not two. Without inner change, there can be no outer change; without collective change, no change matters.

AN INVITATION:
Tending Collective Wounds

It is no wonder that the Earth provides elements that enable you to transform the energies that live inside your body and nervous system field as well as in the collective. Cleansing gives you this opportunity: to hit the reset button on your nervous system, and the collective field of your home, land, and larger community, literally transforming the vibrations that are held within these spaces. Using the power of water, fire, or smoke, we can begin our personal work of tending to collective wounds before initiating participation with other humans—which is an essential next step for healing collective trauma that I hope to prepare you for in this book.

Every culture around the world has cleansing practices and ceremonies as part of their traditions and they most often include the elements of water and fire in the form of smoke. Entering our senses, water and smoke wake up latent energies inside of us, as well as energies held in the collective, and support us in transforming them. Cleansing can include taking an intentional shower or bath, sprinkling water on ourselves or on the Earth as an offering and/or invitation, burning incense, resin, wood, or botanicals, "bathing" or fumigating your home or land in the smoke of herbs, among other practices.

Water has the power to tend collective wounds by waking and removing unwanted energies carried inside of us and held in our environment. Each culture has their own unique practices regarding how water is used to cleanse. Cleansing ceremonies in India that include water frequently take place in rivers known to be sacred and involve immersing and washing your body in the river to cleanse away impurities—your own and also those of your ancestors. In the Himalayas of Nepal where I visit and make an offering of service each year, cleansing ceremonies involve dipping a branch of the artemisia plant into a river or creek and sprinkling onto yourself and the land before ceremony. Christian traditions use Baptism as a form of cleansing by pouring or sprinkling what is known as holy water onto your head. In Judaism, immersion in water is used as a cleansing and purification ceremony.

In addition to water, many cultures burn herbs, resins, and woods in their cleansing ceremonies. In Mesopotamia, the Minoans and Mycenaeans burned labdanum and saffron in smoke cleansing ceremonies. The Assyrians burned cypress, juniper, cedar, boxwood, and fir. The ancient Romans burned cinnamon and rosemary. Ancient Egyptians burned frankincense, myrrh, calamus root, cinnamon, spikenard, and juniper berries. The ancient Chinese burned artemisia, also called mugwort. South Africans burned helichrysum. Indians burned star anise, cedarwood, clove, rose petals, vetiver, valerian, patchouli, sandalwood, agar, and mango wood. Australian Aboriginals burned sandalwood, eucalyptus, and various mints.

Of note, many Native American tribes burned a bundle of white sage as part of their smoke cleansing ceremonies which has come to be known in the West as *smudging* (it should be noted that *smudging* is an English word overlaid onto a sacred Indigenous practice). The smoke from this bundle is known to be a powerful cleanser of people and the environment. Sadly, burning white sage bundles has become commercialized in the United States, so much so that the white sage plant is now endangered. If you are non-Native, I would reconsider using white sage in your own ceremonies so as to protect and honor the culture of Indigenous people as well as the sanctity of the white sage plant. Most cultures around the world do not in fact use herb bundles in their cleansing ceremonies. Instead, they used loose or powdered herbs and resins and were more likely to toss them into a fire or onto hot coals.

Just like all practices I am introducing you to in this book, if you are able, consider learning about the cleansing ceremonies from your own ancestors as these will be more potent for you than any others from another culture. For example, I am of northern European ancestry and will therefore introduce you to an ancient Earth-based Gaelic cleansing ceremony called *saining*, which represents the cleansing ceremony of my own ancestors.

Saining is an old Gaelic cleansing ceremony that involved water, smoke, and fire and is still in use today. My ancestors burned juniper and cedar during their cleansing ceremonies, though juniper is the main herb used in saining today. While this ceremony is held all year round, it is practiced most commonly during the darkest times of the seasonal cycles, i.e. winter, in an effort to ward off sickness and negative energies and to protect the people, plants, animals, and land during this vulnerable time of year. Given that my ancestry is laden with trauma, and that my family and I currently occupy Native land with significant history, I practice saining about once per week in an effort to tend to the energies (and the spirits) of this land.

I find this practice of tending collective trauma to be humbling, reminding me of the power collective energies have over all of us and our lineages. I also find that this practice brings with it inklings of hope, which I feel is a deeply needed resource during these challenging times. So let's begin.

1. **Carve out time.** I recommend setting aside about 30 minutes to an hour to fully engage in this practice.

2. **Gather your element.** Decide if you would like to work with water or smoke from fire. If you choose water, consider visiting a place with water in nature such as a creek, river, lake, or the ocean and asking the beings who live there if you can borrow some of their water for your ceremony (feel into your intuition if you receive a *yes* or a *no*). Or you can pour yourself a small bowl of water from any source to work with. Consider collecting the water the day before and leaving it outside to be kissed in the sunlight or moonlight. Sun energy will charge it with more active energy, strength, and power. Moon energy will charge it with the energy of stillness, restoration, and support clarity.

If you choose to work with fire, I recommend using a charcoal round and dried herbs. Gather these items along with a vessel for the fire to burn safely, a way to create fire (matches, lighter, etc), and water to put out the fire when you are finished. I recommend lighting your charcoal in advance as it typically takes a few minutes until it's ready.

3. **Set an intention.** Start this practice by setting an intention. Ask yourself, what do you need cleansing from? What feels stuck either in you, in your home, or on the land? Do you need to cleanse from negative thoughts or outdated beliefs? Do you need an energetic cleansing of residue from your family or community? Do you need physical cleansing from something that happened to you? Do you need energetic cleansing from the culture and its messaging? Whatever you choose, let this be your intention. State your intention out loud, "I intend to cleanse from _____ so that I can tend to collective wounds."

4. **Call in your supportive guides.** I invite you to begin speaking out loud and calling in all those who support you. Take a look at your resource list from the exercise in Chapter Two, call in these resources. Call in any healthy ancestors for their support, call in animal or plant spirits who support you, call in God, Goddess, Gaia, or who or whatever you look to for guidance. Welcome and say hello to the element of fire or water, whichever element you choose to work with. Ask the element to support you in your intention.

5. **Hold your intention in your heart and mind.** When you are ready, hold your intention in your heart and mind and begin your ceremony. If you are working with water, dip your fingertips into the water and sprinkle the space just in front of you, stating your intention out loud: water please help me cleanse from _____ so that I can tend to collective wounds. Now going clockwise, continue sprinkling water

and naming your intention out loud. Once you have completed the circle nearest you, consider walking the perimeter of your home and land you are occupying in the same manner.

If you are working with the smoke from fire, when the charcoal is ready (as noted by gray spots) and you feel ready, toss a small handful of herbs onto the charcoal, at the same time stating your intention out loud. As the smoke rises, you can "bathe" in it by pulling the smoke toward you and all around you. In this way, you can "wash" your body with the smoke, remembering to repeat your intention out loud each time you toss herbs onto the charcoal. Continue until you have "washed" your whole body in smoke. Afterward, holding your fire-safe vessel, consider walking the perimeter of your home and land you are occupying in the same manner while stating your intention: smoke, please support me in tending to the collective wounds of this home/this land/this community. Continue until you feel an intuitive sense of completion.

6. **Give thanks.** When you feel complete with your cleansing ceremony, offer gratitude out loud to all of the beings you invited in to support you and of course give thanks to the element of fire and/or water for its power of cleansing. If you used fire, saturate it in water and ensure it is completely out before moving on.

Of note: cleansing ceremonies alone will not heal collective trauma however, they will help to move some of the stuck energies that continue to perpetuate the same traumatized fields that many of us live within. This act of service—to you, your ancestors, and also to the Earth and her beings, will make collective healing that much more possible. However, we must remember that while you alone can get this journey of tending collective wounds started, collective healing must ultimately include the participation of the collective. My hope is that once you finish reading this book, you will feel wildly supported, nurtured, and grounded in yourself so much so that you will naturally begin to engage the larger community for the sake of greater healing. My next book will take you deep into this courageous terrain by providing you the very skills you will need on the next leg of your journey.

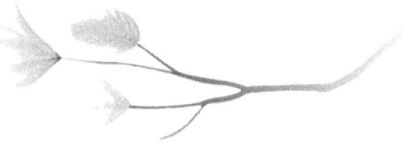

CHAPTER EIGHT:
ORIGINAL TRAUMA

THERE IS ONE TYPE of collective trauma that is pervasive amongst non-Indigenous people that I see makes us more vulnerable to experiencing other traumas. I consider this particular trauma our *original trauma* because when we experience it, this trauma can hold us back in our healing from other traumas. Unlike other traumas, this trauma is insidious, and it has created the very human-centric world that we find coming apart at the edges all around us. Our original trauma is largely the result of colonialism and has left us thinking, feeling, and living as though we are separate from the Earth and her beings. This separation fuels the separation we feel from other humans, from our ancestors, and from the culture.

The moment we started thinking we were separate from the Earth was the moment we unknowingly lost our sense of self and our sense of belonging. Even more damaging than having an insecure attachment style, feeling separate from the Earth creates a fragile foundation that narrows our window of tolerance, decreases our shame tolerance, disconnects us from our powerful sensory system, and leaves us feeling as though *something is always wrong* but unable to put our finger on what it is. The Earth is our root secure base, the mother of all tethers, and when we learn to operate in the world without being in constant explicit relationship with her, we become truly lost.

You see, we humans have evolved so perfectly for the Earth. First, we were bacteria thriving in the waters of the ocean. Then we were fish, followed by amphibians, traversing both water and land. And now we walk upright on the land, breathing in air, yet with our feet planted firmly on the ground. We are evolving and growing interdependently *with* the Earth, her elements, and her rhythmic cycles and seasons. Despite our concrete and our walls and our air conditioning, we are inevitably engulfed in her field. She is under our feet constantly, influencing our bodies, minds, and nervous system.

Having worked for many years in the Indigenous communities of India, Nepal, Thailand, and Burma, I have witnessed that, unlike the Western psyche with which I am accustomed because of my upbringing, this theme of identification with *all of life* and deep, inherent connection to the Earth is a common thread. In fact, this knowledge is not cognitive, it is built into the very fabric of life and identity. The water, air, mountains, plants, and animals do not exist outside of the psyches of the Indigenous people with whom I have worked— they are part of a person's and community's identity.

If you were to trace any culture back to its roots, you would find that all human communities were once a part of Earth-honoring cultures. In fact, as hunter-gatherers, which encompasses at least 90 percent of human history, we held *animistic* views (1). Animism is a way of relating with our world that attributes sentience and offers respect to all life on Earth, including the elements, landscape, and environment. In European history in particular, you will find not only animism but also Druidism, Paganism (a term historically used negatively by Christians but currently making a more positive comeback), Pantheism, and Gaianism—all belief systems that place Earth and her beings at the center of life. The ancient Celts, from which many Westerners have descended, encompassed various tribes who all originated in central Europe and held Earth-honoring traditions like seasonal celebrations and honoring the new and full moons.

I believe this is why there has been, beginning in the late sixties, significant interest for Westerners in Indigenous spirituality and lifestyles. We are searching for a way of being in the world that feels meaningful and not destructive. We have lost connection with our own culture's Earth-honoring traditions and are therefore drawn to cultures that are still living in this balanced and familiar way.

For myself, that was why I was so drawn to Chinese medicine and the psychology of the five elements: because it promotes an Earth-honoring lifestyle that made sense to me and felt strangely familiar. Chinese medicine is based on Taoist philosophy, which is documented somewhere between 8,000 and 9,000 years ago. This philosophy, which also has some religious roots, posits that we humans are not separate from the Earth, but built into the very fabric of the Earth. And just like there are cycles of seasons externally, there are cycles of seasons internally as well. The more our lifestyles are out of alignment with the rhythms and cycles of the Earth, the more imbalanced we become (imbalance in Chinese medicine is what leads to symptoms and dis-ease). This philosophical system, which became the foundation for Chinese medicine, has strongly influenced my lifestyle and my psyche (hence my book, *Everyday Chinese Medicine*).

But as Westerners with colonizer history, though we may be drawn to the beauty and spirituality of Indigenous cultures, we must be careful not to take from these communities. Instead, do explore your own ancestry—even if you have to make guesses and generalizations. The more we continue to take from other cultures, especially Indigenous cultures from whom we have already taken so much, the more disconnected we become from our own ancestry and our own inherent relationship with the Earth and the more harm we continue to perpetuate. And yet, to truly heal, we must start with our relationship with the Earth.

With so many generations between ourselves and our Earth-honoring ancestors who knew they were not separate, in some ways, it may feel as though we are starting our paths anew to repair our relationship with the Earth. To know ourselves as deeply embedded in the fabric of the Earth may feel foreign at first, and yet over time, you will remember this inherent connection and this process will not only be cognitive, but it will also be deeply and unforgettably somatic. We will know in our bones that we are not separate. By tending to this original trauma, you are reclaiming an ancient part of your humanness, thereby restoring your authentic and whole sense of self. Each step of tending will bring you closer and closer to healing your core attachment wounds by earning secure attachment *with the Earth*.

Many theories on earning secure attachment involve healing your attachment wounds by primarily working with other humans. And while I agree that consistent experiences with healthy humans can support you in healing from an insecure attachment style, among a number of other challenges—*there are other ways*. For many of us, our experience of trauma originated from being in relationships with unhealthy humans, and therefore that might not be the best place for many of us to begin our healing journey. For my journey of earning secure attachment, I didn't work with humans until many years into it.

In fact, many of us who struggle with an insecure attachment style may have unconsciously already developed more relationships with the other-than-human beings on Earth. One of my first healthy attachment figures was Orion, a dog I adopted when I was sixteen and moved out of my mother's house. He was an eighty-five-pound brindle Pit-bull rescue, and he was a huge part of my healing from attachment wounds. I have seen plenty of clients and students with insecure attachment styles become dedicated to rescuing animals, gardening, and other practices that are not human-centric. Starting with the Earth, her plants and animals, as well as the spiritual world, can feel much safer than starting our healing work with other humans. This has led me to understand how we humans can earn secure attachment by stepping into a conscious relationship with the Earth and her beings.

AN INVITATION:
Fire Ceremony

Before we can make space for the new, more balanced, more connected and less separate way of being in the world, we have to unlearn and let go of the harmful ways of thinking, feeling, and being we have unconsciously perpetuated. There is no more effective way to to begin this shedding process than to have a fire ceremony. Fire ceremonies have long been a part of all cultures around the world and they all have one theme in common: releasing that which no longer serves us into the fire so it can transform. Fire ceremonies can support us in letting go of negative thoughts, fears, stories, relationships with others, shame, painful memories, and in the work we are doing together—the harmful notion that we are somehow separate from each other and from the Earth.

The element of fire holds the power to cleanse our forests and regenerate our soil, as well as the power to transform and destroy. When used intentionally and with containment, fire can support us in letting go in order to create important space for healing. There are numerous ways to work with the power of fire. During fire ceremonies, you can let things go physically by letting them burn and turn into ash or you can let things go energetically by speaking them aloud or writing them on paper and burning the paper. Fire ceremonies can be done alone or ideally, with people in your community who long for a similar vision of health and balance. Remember, collective healing involves collective participation.

Like all ceremonies, there are specific steps to take to prepare, to execute, and to close a fire ceremony. Here are mine:

1. **Carve out time.** Set aside about one hour for this ceremony. While the ceremony itself may not require a full hour, it is important to give yourself a buffer afterward. You may wind up feeling called to journal or perhaps during your ceremony something will be revealed that presents a call to action. Either way, more time is often better than less time.

2. **Set your intention.** Name your intention for the fire ceremony. In honor of the work that we are doing together, I recommend setting an intention that reflects some of the challenges you discovered in the history of your ancestors as well as the subconscious downloads, cultural messaging, or stories that you may have identified that are no longer serving you. Here are some ideas for intentions:

   + To let go of the shame accumulated from exploring your ancestry
   + To cut ties with an ancestor or person who has a hold on you energetically
   + To let go of the harmful stories you have been carrying around about yourself and the world
   + To let go of some of the ways that you have been influenced by Western culture that are no longer in alignment with who you are now

If none of the above prompts resonate with you, ask yourself, "what do I need to let go of that is no longer serving me?" And see what shows up. Let your intuition be your guide.

3. **Gather objects that represent your intentions.** Find natural, burnable objects that represent this intention such as dead leaves, small sticks, tobacco, herbs such as juniper, cedar, lavender, or resins such as frankincense, myrrh, copal, etc. Or if collecting natural objects is

challenging, consider writing your intentions down, each on its own small slip of paper. As you write down or attribute your intentions, hold the intention in your heart and mind. Gather your objects or pieces of paper and bring them with you as you begin your fire ceremony. Be sure to have access to water to put your fire out when the ceremony is complete.

4. **Light your fire.** Welcome and say hello to the element of fire. Ask the fire element to support you in releasing that which no longer serves you. This does not have to be a giant bonfire and it doesn't even have to be outdoors if that isn't possible. You can have a fire ceremony around a tea light candle if that is all you have access to. As long as it is a safe area with ventilation, and where you will be able to burn your objects or paper, the ceremony will be powerful and effective. At my home we have a small fire pit we use for ceremonies and when I am in the wilderness, we will often use a fire ring.

5. **Call in your supportive guides.** Once your fire is lit, I invite you to begin speaking out loud and calling in all those who support you in resourcing and grounding. Call in any healthy ancestors for their support, call in animal or plant spirits who support you, call in God, Goddess, Gaia, or who or whatever you look to for guidance. Welcome and say hello to who or whatever shows up to support you.

6. **Begin letting go.** Once you have called in your supportive guides and feel grounded in your body and mind, begin the process of working with your intentions in the fire ceremony. Taking one object or piece of paper at a time, I invite you to name out loud what you are releasing. You can even share out loud why you are releasing this and what this means to you if that feels aligned. Just be sure that you are feeling the energy and emotion of what you are asking for support in letting go

of, before you release it into the fire. When you feel ready, place your object or piece of paper in the fire and blow a little bit of breath into it. Repeat this for each intention you set. You might find as you are churning up all that you want to release, that other, unexpected things show up that need releasing, too. Speak those out loud, too and then blow into the fire.

7. **Give thanks.** When you feel complete with your ceremony, give gratitude out loud to all of the beings you invited in to support you in this process and of course give thanks to the element of fire itself for its power of transformation. Saturate your fire in water and ensure the fire is completely out before moving on.

Of note: A fire ceremony doesn't always have to be about letting go. You can have a fire ceremony when things are feeling stuck, when you are calling in something new to your life, or to honor and celebrate an important transition. However, when it comes to severing from the trauma responses that have been carried down through your ancestry and held in the collective, there is no more powerful an element to work with than fire. I recommend holding a fire ceremony each time you cross the threshold into another chapter of your healing journey.

INTERLUDE

DURING MY DARK YEAR of near blindness, I learned more and more about the events leading up to my loss of vision and this life-altering disease I came to befriend, known as Central Serous Choroidal Retinopathy (CSCR) complicated by Choroidal Neovascularization (CNV). I joined online forums, I called doctors who specialize in rare eye diseases in Serbia and in Egypt, and I read medical journals—all with my warped vision. Desperate for answers, I so wanted to keep my vision, if nothing else—in my right eye. It took me a good few months of research before I stumbled upon a third demographic that research has shown is prone to this eye disease: *war veterans*. There wasn't much research available at the time on this particular demographic, not nearly as much research as there was on this disease and its relationship with people who struggle with diabetes and high blood pressure, neither of which I have ever struggled with. But I was determined to find anything I could; there simply *had* to be an explanation.

Then I got to thinking: *why war veterans?* What is it about them and this disease? I wanted to know. And though I am not a war veteran myself, I wondered if there was something similar, a similar biochemistry, that we might share, perhaps?

After many months of working to put the pieces of the puzzle together, I discovered that the link between war veterans and CSCR is the chronic exposure to stress. This chronic exposure leads a person's body to chronic exposure to cortisol in the bloodstream. Cortisol, as you now know, is a hormone that our bodies produce in response to stressful stimuli. When we are frequently exposed to it, it can harm our bodies in a multitude of ways, some obvious and others more insidious.

One of cortisol's negative effects when exposed frequently is to thin the tissues in the body. Therefore, a high-stress and, consequently, high-cortisol lifestyle can lead to the thinning of some of the naturally thinnest membranes in the body first, like the backs of the eyes. When these tissues are thin, they will allow leaking of blood and fluids into the eyes that were not supposed to be allowed in. These fluids can gather around the optic nerve and block vision. And though I am not a veteran myself, the trauma experienced in my childhood, as well as the ancestral and collective trauma I've carried with me through my life, has certainly left residue in my nervous system of a perceived post-war state.

As I write to you today, there is research being published on the link between Type A Personality and Central Serous Retinopathy. Interestingly, what links these two is the same as what links CSCR and war veterans: a high-stress lifestyle, i.e., high cortisol output. Type A Personality (which include traits such as perfectionism, hyper-competitive, fast-paced/impatient, workaholic, and goal-oriented), though historically rewarded by our culture, is more often a survival strategy. I will no longer see Type A traits as something to tout or be proud of. If you are someone who identifies as being Type A, please refer to page 234 to find additional resources for your recovery and healing. (As I write this book, there is similar research being done on the link between trauma and attention-deficit/hyperactivity disorder (ADHD) in both adults and children. In the last decade of practicing holistic medicine in my clinic, these are two experiences that I have noted have an extremely high correlation—one that I have never been able to ignore. See page 234 for additional information).

Despite many years of therapy and education, traumatic experiences from my past that were still living in my nervous system came back around full circle no longer *asking* for my attention—but rather, demanding it. I needed to slow down, or else. I needed to pay attention to my body, or else. While there are many reasons to remain on edge in today's society, I no longer wanted the old feedback loop from my traumatized nervous system to be the reason. I wanted to heal. Not only my vision, but the reason I lost my vision. I wanted to become less vulnerable, more resourceful, and resilient.

Healing requires severing from that which is no longer in service of your life and its path. However, severance is not about choice, or kindness, or good timing. Severance does not apologize for what she takes, nor what lies in her aftermath. Just like autumn returning each year to cool the air and take our leaves, severance is a completely natural, rhythmic, and necessary process—even when she catches us off guard, even when what she takes feels wildly unfair. Severance is a gatekeeper of balance after all, the fire that destroyed so that the forest could regenerate.

Before losing my vision, I was living completely out of balance. I had become so comfortable with chaos, with hyperfunctioning, with the unrelenting busyness we all know so well. I was a bundle of trauma responses, filling any perceived spaciousness with just one more thing to do and operating as though I was separate from everyone else, as though I was leading my own one-woman army. I had no idea the toll it would take.

First, severance took my vision. But she was only getting started. After my experience of near-blindness on that plane, I spent the next eighteen months on a rigorous healing journey that forced me to let go of nearly everything that once felt familiar and comforting. I felt tossed out to sea with no shore in sight. *Which way do I swim?* Even my survival strategies born out of my attachment wounds were put to the test; there was no fleeing. Sitting with myself in that dark space (literally and figuratively), everything that was not rooted in the dark, rich soil of the Earth was turned to ash.

I realized I had to let go of friendships; even long-held ones that I couldn't imagine my life without. These were brothers and sisters who I once held so near and dear only to discover that we were not bonded in a deep, soul-level connection, we were bonded by our trauma, by our wounding. And when that wounding began to transform, so did the friendships. *Who would I become without these friendships?*

I had to let go of relationships with colleagues because those relationships were based on similar expressions of workaholism and scarcity mentality. When I could no longer muster up the energy for happy hours or yoga classes, when I began having different needs and could not keep up the same pace, nor save face, we grew apart. Projects that I had created, had stood behind, all the causes I had been saying yes to for so many years, began to whittle and dissolve without my tending. *Who would I become without my work?*

I had to let go of family members who, when they were in my life, needed more than I was able to give. More familiar with being in a caregiver role for my family, when I was finally the one in need, our relationships were turned upside down. The tidal waves of their addictions and their rollercoaster of mental and physical health issues were no longer something I had the bandwidth for. *Who would I become without my family?*

My typical presentation and participation in the world had to be let go. I simply did not have the internal resources to spend. I could not see my usual load of patients each week, I could not send out my usual newsletters or craft my social posts. I could not go out into the world knowing I was doing everything I can to end unnecessary suffering. Making plans and directing projects were going to be the death of me. *Who would I become without participating so fully in society?*

As I let go of these things and sat with the questions themselves, I became untethered to my former self. *This is what I mean by severance.* On this journey of tending the unhealed trauma, we will stumble across parts of ourselves—like clothes in our closet that don't fit anymore. We will see the relationships and hear the stories that continue to reinforce this now incongruent way of living. And though it may feel wildly painful and disorienting, we will know—*they must go.*

When we have unhealed trauma living in our nervous systems, we create a life based on the rules this unhealed trauma has crafted for us. These rules often come out of a fear, scarcity, and a shame-based way of living. The decisions we make for our lives, however big or small, often lead us to find a soft, wounded core that, if tended, would unravel into a completely different life. This is why severance can be so scary. Who do we become without our stories, without our friendships, without our human families, and without our culture?

Losing my vision taught me that I needed to sever from the story of who

I had become. After this experience of nearly going blind, I was forced "off." It was not a dark night of the soul—*it was a dark year of the soul*. Something I never would have signed up for but without it, I never would have had my psyche so undone (a terrifying but necessary process). I needed a deep soul-level examination, a severance of all things familiar, and a forced surrender to the dark waters of my oncoming healing journey. I *needed* to shed all that I had been holding on to so that I could see my raw, bare body underneath the surface and listen—actually listen to her for the first time in a great while.

If I didn't pause long enough to do just that, I would be giving my power away to the culture and its messaging of *just pick yourself up by your bootstraps and keep moving, honey*. I needed to bow to this next chapter, this letting go; to honor it as part of my process of growth and transformation. To trust it. *I had to let go of what I thought I knew to discover what I knew in my bones.* I needed to be without distraction and to be close to the Earth for answers.

One evening I filled the back of my Subaru with remnants of a dead tree taken down in my yard the year prior, several gallons of water, my notebook, and a couple of pens. I drove up into the mountains to one of my favorite campsites on unincorporated land in the Roosevelt National Forest, where I knew there wouldn't be a soul in sight. The moon was nearly full, and my heart was heavy. I *needed* a fire ceremony. I needed to honor all I had learned over the last year and to say goodbye to this chapter in my life. As difficult as it was, I needed to welcome severance as a friend. I needed to trust her.

As the sun was setting, I began pulling the wood out of the trunk of my car and building my fire in the fire ring. The air was dry, and there was only the tiniest breeze I could hear tickling the grasses behind me. A little paper from my journal proved to be the only kindling needed to get the fire blazing. The moon, in its full glory, sat just above the valley, and all became quiet except for the crackling of the fire at my feet.

I brought out my pen and paper and began writing so that I could clarify my intention:

I am exhausted, and I nearly lost my vision because I kept saying yes and offering myself up to others and to my work. I have been moving so fast and taking so much on. I have been working so hard for so long. Do I really need to work this hard? Am I only valuable when I am available to and caring for others? And if I can't work, will I become powerless and dependent? I am out of integrity with myself and my priorities are all jumbled up. I feel like I need to move fast and do it all or else everything will fall apart. I am overextended in friendships that aren't nourishing me back. If I don't appease those around me, I will end up alone.

I read my words aloud, over and over again, so I could really drink in where I was emotionally at the time. Like a snake outgrowing her skin, I needed to shed these stories so that I could see what was genuine underneath.

I tore up the paper that I had been writing my intentions on and held them in my hand. One at a time:

I don't want to live my life exhausted anymore.

I threw the piece of paper into the fire and blew on it until I saw the sparks and felt the fire grow a little warmer.

I don't want to move so fast anymore.

I threw that piece of paper into the fire and blew once again.

I don't want to work so hard anymore.

Then that piece of paper went in.

I don't want to live at the mercy of others.

And in it went.

I don't want to live my trauma responses anymore.

Tossing it in.

I don't want to live with my ancestors' trauma responses anymore.

Then that piece of paper went in.

I don't want to be so vulnerable to the collective trauma in the world.

In it went.

I deserve healing, authentic expression, freedom, and joy. I belong. I am resilient.

Burn baby, burn.

And I continued in this manner until all the paper that needed to be burned was burned and all that needed to be let go was spoken to. I felt complete. After all that shedding, I felt ready for the next chapter. I let go of *so much* that night. When I doused the fire and packed up my car, I felt cleared out, empty. I even felt a tickle of joy coursing through my veins. I laughed out loud on my way down the mountain as I couldn't even find anything to feel anxious about. And believe me, I tried. That was foreign and deserving of celebration.

At times on my healing journey, I needed to turn away from the culture so that I could *feel* myself and find myself once again. This time was different, this was a great shedding. Surprisingly, there was a certain kind of freedom living on the other end of severance. A freedom, like an undifferentiated cell, where I was gifted the opportunity to reenter my life like a blank slate...*tabula rasa*. Not that there weren't layers upon layers of grief yet to go through to get there.

PART THREE

YOU ARE NOT SEPARATE

"Sometimes I wake up & have to remind myself: 'There is nothing wrong with me. I have patterns to unlearn, new behaviors to embody and wounds to heal. But there is nothing wrong with the core of me and who I am. I am unlearning generations of harm and remembering love. It takes time."

—Yolo Akili

TIME AND TIME AGAIN, I have seen humans blossom and heal from even extreme trauma by cultivating and sustaining their relationship with the Earth and her beings. Through gentle daily relational practices and wilderness experiences, I have witnessed the same benefits of earning secure attachment with healthy humans become readily available—if not more so, in relating with the Earth and her beings. There are five essential steps I have found that work to support you in beginning your journey of remembering we are not separate while earning secure attachment with the Earth. I will take you through each of these steps in Part Three. This is your time of initiation, the dismantling before the reassembling. If you can *go all in* with the following material, you will find that you carry a gift so powerful, you can change the course of humanity.

.

CHAPTER NINE:

ESTABLISHING YOUR
SECURE BASE

I HOLD STRONGLY THE BELIEF that everything in this world is sacred and that each one of us has the opportunity to connect with sacred places of our own on the Earth, places where we feel at "home," inside ourselves. Places that align so perfectly with our nervous system field and that attune to us; places where we ground and settle down easily inside. Places that invite us to let go of the energies of society, to drop our boundaries, and be in direct contact with the land in a way that feels safe, and that our nervous system responds to with a big "ahhhhhh." These sacred places, once we get to know them, can become a powerful source of energy for us, expediting the healing of our attachment wounds, and supporting us to land more fully in our bodies. Step one of earning secure attachment with the Earth involves remembering our relationship with the land by finding our unique sacred places in her landscape and tending to them.

Many of us already have a place or *several places* like this on the Earth. I had a special tree at this park that I always felt drawn to when I was a teenager. And a bench by a lake in the city of Richmond when I was in my early twenties. And a field by the river near an old, abandoned Virginia dairy farm.

Plus, I've always felt a special attachment to an isolated beach not far from my childhood home and would even find myself visiting this place in my dreams. These were all special places that I was naturally drawn to and could spend hours there without needing distraction. When I would go back home after spending time at these special places, I frequently felt better in my body and more grounded in my life.

If you had asked me why or what it is I liked about these places years ago, I would have probably told you I have no idea—that I just felt really at home when I was there. But now I know that there is a *resonance* in these places that I feel and this resonance enables me to shed the energies/vibrations that are not serving me and to plug back into the powerful, sustaining energies and vibrations of the Earth. Resonance is a type of deep connection, a reflection of *I'm picking up what you are putting down*, and otherwise shared vibrations with another being or environment. When you feel resonance, you also likely feel familiarity, comfort, and safety.

It is not surprising to know that different places on Earth will evoke different energies in you. Think of the difference between sitting low in a valley by a trickling creek versus sitting high up on a mountaintop with a grand view. Both places can be remarkably powerful, and yet both can conjure different energies from the Earth and resonate with different energies inside of you.

We all need to have these sacred places available to us where we can be in direct contact with the Earth—a place that we have grown to know so well that it is almost like another limb. And also a place that has grown to know us so well that not all of the inhabitants dash off the moment we arrive; a place that encourages us to drop in and remember we are not separate. These places become like deep wells for us to draw strength and connection from. If you don't already have a place that has come to mind as you've been reading, I will walk you through the steps of finding your own secure base/sacred place on Earth so you can begin your process of earning secure attachment. With this attachment, you have the opportunity to regulate and repattern your nervous system no matter where you find yourself on the planet; the Earth is consistently available and nonjudgmental, and trust me when I say, she cannot wait for you to find your way back home to her.

1. **Locate a sacred place.** Ideally, you have at least one place you can walk to, either from your home, from work, or from another place you frequently visit. It doesn't have to be a pristine place like a national park or botanical garden, away from all other humans; however, a place with fewer distractions is best, and a place with direct contact with the Earth (ideally not a balcony unless that is all you have at the moment). As you get familiar with this practice of locating your sacred places, you will naturally find many sacred places all around you.

2. **Become a regular.** Once you have located a space, start by visiting this place every day or as often as you can (at least a few times each week initially). Plan to spend a *minimum* of twenty minutes during each visit. I have found that twenty minutes is often just enough time for most of us to slow down and feel our feet on the Earth (you may find that you need far more than twenty minutes, especially at first and then over time, you may find that you need less).

3. **Orient to your inner landscape.** Get cozy by having a seat or lying down. Once you have physically arrived, to help you arrive more fully in your body and psyche—consider scanning your body from head to toe in your mind's eye. As you scan, try to give each part of your body a little bit of attention. Notice where in your body you are having sensation. If you can, identify what kind of sensation: dull, heavy, light, fluttery, etc. Notice if there is any particular kind of energy or emotion you have brought with you to this place today: Are you feeling open and warm? Cold and shutdown? Are you feeling over-whelmed? Are you feeling busy and full? Are you tired and cranky? No judgment—just noticing.

4. **Orient to the outer landscape.** Now that you have noticed what is happening within you, open your eyes and take a look around to see what is happening around you in this place. Notice the particular kind of Earth you are sitting on. Is it dry? Or wet? Is it grassy or mulched? Look around you; are trees or plants near? Do you recognize any of them? What about people or animals? What kind of life lives there? It might be difficult on your first few visits to sense the life there. Often when we come into natural places with our frazzled nervous system vibrations and our hard-staring eyes, all the living creatures will run for their lives. We can't blame them—we humans can be intense. But just as you will get used to this new place, the new place and its habitants will get used to you, too. They will begin returning much quicker after your arrival, especially as your nervous system entrains to the land and ecosystem.

5. **Breathe with the local plants.** Now that you have oriented our senses, take a few deep breaths. I recommend the plant breathing invitation in Chapter One. If you catch your mind wandering off and back to work or back to other human "stuff," just come back to your breath.

6. **Notice any changes.** Once you've done at least ten rounds of plant breathing, check in again with your body. What do you notice? What, if anything, has shifted since you first arrived? Are you gaining more sensation or less? Are you feeling more relaxed or less? Have any critters come around? Just notice; no need to analyze or judge your experience.

The more you visit this place, just like visiting with friends, you will naturally develop a kinship. The more you reveal to this place through imagery, words, or bodily sensation, the more this place will reveal to you. Give it some time.

And just as you assess a new friendship, assess this new place. How well do you get along? Do you find yourself thinking about this place and excited to go visit? Listen to your body for cues. You may need to go through this exercise with a few different places. Sometimes when I find a new, sacred place in nature, I will go through this exercise facing different directions each time so that I can find the perfect alignment between my body and the place I have chosen (or has chosen me). I have also experimented with the edges of different bodies of water. I have sat on the north side of a lake to go through these steps and then also tried the east, south, and west sides of the lake to look for *resonance within my being.*

Being in a sacred place on the Earth, just like being in a temple or visiting an Indigenous sacred site, is an invitation for your nervous system to be dominated by a larger energy force. Once you have established your sacred place, your nervous system will do the unwinding for you if you just continue to visit and spend agenda-less time there.

Visit in all the different seasons, in all the different weather patterns as well as in all of *your* different seasons and weather patterns (moods, states of mind, etc.). Burn your favorite herbs there, drink your favorite teas there, and play your favorite games there. Know that sometimes it will feel like nothing is happening at all, but lean on your trust in me for the time being—your nervous system is gathering loads of information in this rhythmic revisiting, and the same is happening for the Earth. Get to know this part of the Earth so that its energy becomes ingrained in you. You will know this happens when you find yourself able to conjure this place in your mind while you are not physically present at your sacred place, and yet your nervous system is benefitting as though it is physically present on the land. And before you know it, you will sit down in your sacred place and the animal beings, who also call this place home, will stay with you because your nervous system attunes and entrains to the space so quickly.

Once you have found and visited your sacred space several times, try this at home when you have fewer distractions: sit or lie down and close your eyes for a mini-meditation. Imagine you are in your sacred place: What do you hear? What do you smell? What do you see? Bring the detailed features of your sacred place into your meditation. And perhaps practice your plant breathing with your place in your mind's eye. Practice this at your workplace when you need to take a break but can't. Or, if you are experiencing something challenging, call on the power of your sacred place until you feel an energetic shift. Over time, what you will notice is that your sacred place can be called upon anytime, day or night. It is like a friend who is always there; you just have to remember to invite her over. This exercise will enable your sacred place to become a resource you have access to no matter where you are.

And finally, celebrate! You have just gathered another amazing personal resource to add to your growing list from the exercise in Chapter Two. Keep your sacred place in your heart and mind, and remember to visit it often, physically and also energetically. And continue exploring and adding sacred places to your personal resources. Each time you travel or visit a new place, look for these sacred places all around you—they are there, they want to be found.

A note on behalf of the Earth: Given how powerful this resource is that lies just beneath our feet, I am shocked that so many are able to violate the Earth and her resources. But many of us do it without even knowing it (carbon footprint, industrial farming, and agriculture, etc.). Needless to say, stepping back into a relationship with the Earth will naturally bring about an energy of advocacy. And Mother Earth needs our advocacy and stewardship now more than ever. So whenever I am in direct contact with her, I am also sensing the delight that she and her beings must be feeling in return for having a being who is consciously relating with her. Indeed this is a win for us all.

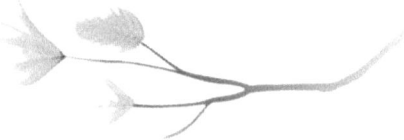

CHAPTER TEN:

DISCOVERING YOUR
PLANT ALLIES

GATHERERS HAD A DEEPLY INTIMATE relationship with plants. They were the keepers of the healing power of plants and used their instincts to locate and identify them in the landscape and to use them both as food and as medicine. From generation to generation, they passed on the wisdom of identification, ethical harvesting, and preparation. In fact, much of our gatherer psyche was dedicated to plant knowledge. Plants were used in our ceremonies and in all types of healing, accompanying us at births and also during sickness and death. Plants have long been a part of our identity, and they are powerful teachers that can hold sacred space for healing. Linda Hogan, Chickasaw poet and novelist, reminds us that, "In most Indigenous creation stories, humans were the last ones created. Around us are many teachers," she says, referring to the plants.

Each plant carries medicine within it, for the Earth or for other beings. Sometimes the medicine is physical medicine, the way the bark of the cinchona tree carries anti-malaria medicine within it. Though consuming plants for their physical medicines is one way to learn about them, they contain other medicines as well, some of which are not for human consumption or not for humans at all. Some plants are medicine for the Earth, growing to balance an ecosystem or to nourish the other-than-human world. Plants also carry spiritual or energetic medicine, the way a pasque flower relieves feelings of emotional burden and heartache when you drink her flower essence or call upon her energy to enter your body. Understanding the energetic properties and potency of plants and having a strong, respectful, personal relationship with them infuses you with extraordinary wisdom and ancient power.

Each one of us has what I like to call *plant allies*. Robin Wall Kimmerer, Potawatomi botanist and author of *Braiding Sweetgrass,* shares in her book, "In some Native languages, the term for plants translates to 'those who take care of us.'" These are plants that you innately share a resonance with, who have been likely guiding you throughout your life—sometimes always the same plants, and other times new plant allies show up, especially during challenges and transitions. These are often plants you feel naturally drawn to—perhaps a plant you frequently notice on your walk through the neighborhood or a plant that always manages to make its way, potted into your home or between the cracks of your sidewalk. Or maybe there is a tea you drink that you can't seem to get enough of? Take a look around you. Do you see any plants in your environment? Do you feel any special kinship with or curiosity about these plants?

Imagine for a moment that all the plants around you—the house plants, the plants covering your lawn or your balcony, the plants you see on your way into the office—imagine there was consciousness on the other end. Imagine they were all familiar with you, they knew your name, and they knew what you were up to on a daily basis, and whichever emotional state you were feeling at any given moment. Imagine that they could change their energies to help you manage your own energy. What if you were having a difficult day and you could simply call on juniper or elderberry to support you in feeling more at ease, more grounded, more at home in yourself, and more clear about how to move forward?

This is what humans have been doing for thousands of years: communicating with plants. We have been giving and receiving with the plant queendom for healing, protection, wisdom, and divination since the beginning of time (1).

I can vividly remember the first time I learned about communicating with plants. I was in my twenties, studying with a shamanic teacher in Boulder, Colorado, at Naropa University, and I felt sure this teacher was on hallucinogens. She was telling us that we could learn to conjure up plant medicine in our minds and use it to heal whatever ails our loved ones or—even if our loved ones or the plants were far away. If it weren't for the fact that I was getting credit for taking the course, I may have never returned after the first class, as it felt so far from my paradigm at the time.

But as I set my critical brain aside and went along with her for the ride, a part of my brain—an old, old part that had been closed for some time due to my personal traumas and the toxic framework laid on me by the culture—began to shift and open up. I started to be able to feel the *possibility* of the healing power of plants—in their energetic form—not even in their physical form, as that came later through my studies in herbal medicine.

Eventually as I completed my training with this shamanic teacher, I could simply think of a plant and a certain part of my body would light up, letting me know what part of my body (or others' bodies) could be helped by this plant. I was stunned and also overjoyed to be let in on this ancient secret. Don't worry, I will help you remember these skills so you, too, can have access to this incredible and abundant resource as well as open these long-since-closed places in your own psyche. These places have been longing for you to open them. I want to bring you back into this ancient circle of wisdom, this abundant resource, so that you can begin to feel who your plant allies might be and start strengthening those relationships right away. This is the next step to remembering you are not separate, all the while earning secure attachment with the Earth. Let's get started.

1. **Choose a plant to connect with.** Perhaps you already have some inkling—perhaps there is a plant that you always feel drawn to in your

landscape or a tree that you love to sit under or look at. What about a plant that is intriguing to you from your sacred space? Or maybe there is a houseplant that somehow always makes its way to you—even when you move far away—she manages to show up. Whatever the plant or tree is, I want you to pick one for now so you can focus your intention and find out why she keeps showing up for you and if she is in fact one of your powerful resources.

If you happen to live near a park, have access to a yard, or even better—a wild place, I recommend choosing a plant in its natural habitat versus a houseplant as I have found that the potency of the plant medicine when its roots are deep in the Earth to be much stronger than when potted. However, for many of us, a houseplant is the easiest and only option—and that's okay, too. Connecting to houseplants can sometimes require more skill because of this difference. Above all, I want you to be able to visit this plant frequently, so don't choose a plant that is far away or difficult to get to—as tempting as that may be.

2. **Become a regular.** Once you have chosen your plant (or your plant has chosen you), I want you to begin an almost daily practice of visiting this plant. Bring a journal, a pen, a blanket or chair—whatever will keep you comfortable—so that you can visit this plant friend as frequently as possible and in all kinds of weather (remember, internal and external weather changes). Always greet with a "hello" and close with a "good-bye," just as you would with a human friend. As much as you are able, refrain from looking this plant up in any other sources until you have finished all the steps in this exercise. Another person's interpretation of this plant and its uses may not be the same wisdom you will gain from connecting directly with this plant.

3. **Get to know her physically.** When you sit with your plant, feel free to inspect her. First, look at her leaves, her flowers, her stems, limbs, or bark. Examine her thoroughly. What colors do you see, and what shades of those colors? Notice how she has grown—has it been an easy, straight shot toward the sun for her? Or has she had to navigate through human stuff like concrete or shadows of buildings? Does she lean left or right? Has she had to rely on other plants or objects to find her way toward the sun? Has one side of her grown more than the other? Notice everything you can about her visually and either write it out in your journal or draw her in your journal. Of note, your drawing does not have to attempt to mimic her exactly. It could be a completely abstract drawing—as long as it makes sense to you and when you look at the drawing, you know exactly which plant you are referring to.

4. **Explore her scent.** On your second visit, I want you to drop into your olfactory sense and smell her. Lean in and smell her in her natural state. Smell her root area, her bark or stems, smell her leaves, and most certainly—smell her flowers if she has them out. You may find that gently rubbing these areas of her physical form will release her smells if you are having trouble smelling her (or if she is withholding). A gentle rub on her leaf or a swipe with the tips of your fingers through the soil at her roots will give you that information. Write down what you discover.

5. **Explore her sound.** On your third visit, I want you to drop into your auditory sense and listen to her. Sit close enough that you are able to hear her. Does she make any sounds? When the wind blows, do you hear any quaking of her leaves or ruffling of her petals? Is she saying anything to you? If she were to sing a song, what would her voice sound like? Write it down.

6. **Explore her somatic impact.** On your fourth visit, I want you to drop into *your* full-body felt sense while you are with her. By now, she is getting used to you, and you are getting used to her, so there is a familiarity forming that is not only cognitive. When you sit down next to her, what do you notice in your body? Do you feel relaxed and calm? Or excited and energized? Is there anywhere in your body that wakes up when you are near her? Is there anywhere in your body that feels soothed by being in her presence? Write it down.

7. **Share some part of yourself.** On your fifth visit, I want you to share a little bit about yourself out loud. Plants are very much sensitive beings and as such, they respond to even the subtlest energy in their environment—even thoughts—as much as they respond to physical contact. If ever you need evidence of this, consider reading *The Secret Life of Plants* by Peter Tompkins and Christopher Bird. On this visit, tell your plant friend about an experience you are currently going through or one from the past. Let it be a story that has significance to you. Once you have shared this with your plant friend, sit quietly and listen. Do you hear any response? What do you feel in your body after sharing and then now listening? Do you have any impulses? Write it down.

The amazing thing about plant allies is that the stronger a relationship you have with them in their physical form, the more potent their medicine becomes in its energetic form. Eventually, you won't need to be in proximity to the plant in order to feel connected or (with permission from the plant) to use its medicine.

From this point forward, I encourage you to visit your plant ally as frequently as possible. Even if it feels like nothing is happening, keep going to visit the plant. Remember, part of recovering from unhealed trauma is that your nervous system has become more attuned to chaos and more alarmed by slowness. This is a healing journey to repattern your nervous system for connection, and it doesn't happen overnight. Just to give you an example, when I was getting to know the mullein plant, I visited her every day for almost an entire year. Sometimes the lack of stimulation would enable me to fall asleep while I was visiting her—a sure sign of deep relaxation.

Each time you visit your plant ally, share more about yourself, another story or something you are currently going through. Let this plant into your world—but after your share, remember to always listen. Plants are wise beings and deserve space to feel and communicate—the same space you would give to a human friend. It would be unkind to just dump on them and walk away. Notice any changes in the inner and outer landscape after you share.

Now that you have gotten to know this plant through your own body and its powerful senses, I recommend doing some research to learn more about the science and folklore of this plant. What is its scientific name? Where is it native to? What is unique about this plant? What are its known nutritional and medicinal uses? Does it belong to a particular traditional medical system? Learn as much as you like and use that knowledge to infuse the knowledge that you have already gathered about the plant using your own sensory system. You might be surprised at how much these two ways of gathering information (using your body as one source and either books, articles, or the internet as another source) will land you in very similar terrain. Many people discover as they are learning about plants and their medicines, they feel surprisingly nourished, excited, and even somewhat of a familiarity with the plants. I believe this is because of our gatherer history and the wisdom housed deep in our brain stems.

Whichever plants show up for you, they are now a part of your personal resources. Even if the plant is not physically nearby, you can easily call on the energy of the plant to step forward, most especially during challenging times, and keep calling on her until you can feel the shift in your own energy when the plant "arrives." Your plant allies are there for you no matter what state of mind you are in. Be on the lookout daily for plant allies, as you likely have many, many more who are excitedly waiting to connect with *you*.

I once had a student named Sarah who kept noticing mullein around her each time she went on a walk or drove down the highway. Because she felt like this plant was everywhere and, therefore, it didn't feel as special to her as the more rare and beautiful plants she spotted, and she didn't feel much like connecting with this plant and exploring its medicine. Then one day, Sarah joined me on a forest walk in the foothills of the Rocky Mountains, where I regularly take students on a tour of the local medicinal plants. Lo and behold, halfway through the walk, Sarah tripped on a stalk of mullein, falling and twisting her ankle. We all stopped to check in and to offer support. This was when she told me how she keeps seeing mullein everywhere but that she hasn't felt called to connect with it.

"I think it's possible this plant is trying to connect with you, Sarah," I said.

With a swollen, aching ankle, Sarah decided to stay put, right next to mullein, while the group continued on our walk—knowing we would circle back around and collect her on our way back to the trailhead.

While we were away, Sarah dropped into her body and senses to get to know this plant that seems to be unrelenting in its presence. "Who are you?" she wondered.

As our group finished our walk together and circled back around, we found Sarah sitting in the same exact place on the side of the trail, except with tears streaming down her face.

"Sarah, are you okay?" I asked.

"I'm perfect," she answered with sniffles and a smile. Keeping her eyes closed, clearly focusing her attention internally. "I think I just found

a plant ally," she said while bursting into tears. Sarah went on to share with our group some of the medicine that mullein had shared with her.

Sarah told us that she placed her hand on mullein's furry leaf and was immediately overcome with grief. The tears started pouring down her face and she wasn't sure what that was about as there didn't seem to be a story attached to the grief. Unafraid, she let the grief wash over her. The grief felt big, as though she was grieving for something so much larger than herself. Sarah was able to stay with it, to let it move through what felt like every cell in her body.

Then, suddenly, she felt a sense of gratitude and relief wash over her. Her heart no longer felt heavy; her chest felt as though it had been cracked open; she felt as though she could finally breathe. She breathed and breathed, pulling the fresh mountain air deep into her lungs.

Still with her eyes closed, she felt a shift in the environment. Unable to sense what it was, using her hearing and felt sense, she opened her eyes to see a large butterfly had landed on the mullein plant next to her hand. Sarah was overcome with delight and awe. She felt soothed by the presence of the butterfly, as though it was a part of the medicine of mullein. Mullein seemed to teach her about the importance of grief, she thought, trusting its heaviness and movement through her body, her lungs, and her tears. The butterfly seemed to remind her of grief's other half: tenderness, gentleness, love, and awe.

Returning from our walk, Sarah decided to learn more about the history and uses of mullein. It was of no surprise to her to learn that many Native American communities used the leaves of mullein medicinally to clear out the respiratory system by both making tea as well as smoking it. In Chinese medicine, she also discovered the lungs are considered home to our grief. Lastly, Sarah discovered that mullein is native to Europe, just like her ancestors. She felt a kinship with this plant that continues to this day.

CHAPTER ELEVEN:
WELCOMING ANIMALS AS TEACHER

JUST LIKE PLANTS, ANIMALS are all around us, from insects to birds to fish to amphibians and mammals, and we are surrounded by their life-forms permeating our energy fields constantly. Many of us even choose to have animals as pets typically because we feel a resonance with their unique energy. We all know at least a few "dog-people," and "cat-people," and so on.

Native hunters had a deeply intimate relationship with animals. They were masters at attuning to the rhythms and behaviors of animals, tracking them and hunting them for food, clothing, and medicine. They used their instincts to locate their habitats and keep their communities fed and safe.

From generation to generation, hunters passed on the wisdom of ethical hunting and meat preparation. In fact, much of our hunter psyche was dedicated to animal knowledge. Animals were used sacrificially in our ceremonies and in many types of healing, including using certain parts of an animal's body to heal certain parts of human's bodies. As John Madson says, "I do not hunt for the joy of killing but for the joy of living, and the inexpressible pleasure of mingling my life however briefly, with that of a wild creature that I respect, admire and value." Animals have long been a part of our identity, and they are powerful teachers for us.

Rebuilding strong relationships with the animal world serves us in many ways. For one, many of our wounds have involved other humans, therefore often, being in relationship with the animal world feels safer than being in relationship with other humans. Second, animals can become attachment figures for us and help us along our path to earning secure attachment. Pets, in particular, can become an incredibly consistent presence in our lives, greeting us each time we walk in the door and providing comfort, friendship, and even protection when we feel unsafe. These rhythmic and consistent behaviors make them excellent healers. Third, the more we get to know animals and their unique characteristics and quirks, the more compassion we will naturally develop for humans and their characteristics and quirks. Lastly, being able to call on the energetic power of our animal teachers can support us in staying regulated in our nervous systems and resourced during challenging times. Imagine, just like when we open ourselves to the plant world, if you were having a challenging day and you could call on the wisdom of owl or the strength of bear? What if simply calling on them provided you with the energy and foresight you needed to get through the challenging experience?

However, animals provide so much more than all of this. Animals are sovereign beings who have a spiritual nature as well as a physical one (just like plants and humans). And when they show up unannounced in our lives, it is worth investigating their energetic nature to see what we might learn from them. Have you ever found a stray dog or cat or injured bird right at the exact moment that you were struggling to feel connection and compassion? Or have you ever been deep in thought only to have a butterfly, or a bird, come linger right in front of your face for a moment—pulling you out of your thoughts and into the present moment? Just like plants, we have animals that show up to teach us lessons and to help us heal. It is, however, up to us to determine what that teaching is. Animals can help us find hidden parts of ourselves, cultivate courage when we need it, and guide us through the most difficult time of our lives.

I have found the animals we each resonate with (even if they are animals like whales—who typically don't become pets) say a lot about who we are and the kinds of energy we are calling in. And here's the catch, if a whale teacher is showing up for you in your life, the medicine it is carrying might not be the same medicine it carries for another person who is also having the whale teacher show up. That is why it is of utmost importance that you learn to read the signs of your animal teachers for yourself, . Reading the signs involves, you guessed it—listening to the wisdom of your body and its powerful sensory system.

Some animals may show up physically, whereas others may show up energetically through dreams or visions. I have had animals physically show up for me, such as horses, foxes, northern flickers, and great horned owls. Spiritually, through dreams and visions, I have had different animals show up that I had yet to meet in real time, such as elephants (though I have since been blessed enough to have many experiences with elephants in physical form).

Different animals may show up for you at different times of your life. I had several years when fox and bear were physically showing up in my life and then several years when I did not catch a glimpse of them except in my dreams. And yet when I think back to those times when fox and bear were more present, it was the perfect time for me to be intermingling with both of their spiritual medicines. For me, fox showed up to teach me about taking my time in the decision-making process and to see the decisions from all angles (I had a big school decision in my life at the time that I needed to make, and I was feeling pressure about how to respond). Bear appeared for me to remind me to take that deeper care for myself—to become *mama bear* to myself, set clear boundaries, and be okay with simplicity for a while.

As you have been reading about animal teachers, you might already have an animal that you've noticed continues to show up in your life. The truth is, we all do. It's only that some of us are paying more attention than others. Perhaps you continue to pull the same animal totem card from the deck at your local bookstore or apothecary. If you are an artist, you may find yourself having animal themes in your creations. Regardless of how they show up for you, if they are showing up—I recommend exploring their meaning for you in the following invitation. If you have several animal teachers who continue to appear for you, I recommend choosing only one at a time to start exploring.

1. **Find an animal.** Choose an animal teacher in your life, one who has shown up recently (i.e., in the last month or so). Energetically bring this animal teacher into your space as though they are standing right in front of you. Begin writing down all the adjectives that you associate with this animal being.

2. **What interests you about this animal?** Next, write down a few sentences about what intrigues you most about this animal. Think about things you already know about this animal rather than looking them up. Remember, this is making meaning for *you*.

3. **What relationship do you have with this animal?** How does this animal show up for you? Does it come to you in your dreams? Or do you spot this animal in the wild? Does someone special in your life keep mentioning it to you? What are the circumstances that surround this animal's presence in your life, dreams, or otherwise?

4. **What was happening in your life when this animal first appeared?** Were you going through something important in your life? A transition? On the precipice of a big decision? Were you struggling or celebrating something?

5. **How does your psyche, body, and spirit change in the physical or energetic presence of this animal?** What shifts in you while in the presence of this animal? How does your body and psyche change? Do you feel more relaxed? Energized? At home inside yourself? Do you feel a part of your body or psyche light up? Write these things down as they are perhaps the most important part of the exercise.

Once you have an idea of who your animal teachers are, I recommend bringing them even more into your life by practicing some of the following:

+ **Decorate your world with reminders of them.** Photographs, poetry, paintings, wallpaper on your computer or phone, you name it. Keep images of these special animal teachers so that you remember them and their energy often.

+ **Embody their qualities and attributes.** With owls, for example, you could sit outside at night and observe the sights and sounds. With fox, for example, you could go on a walk in the woods, pretending to stalk prey trying not to be seen or heard.

+ **Build a relationship with your animal teacher.** Get to know them. You could even imagine them standing behind you or in front of you as you go about your day—whichever feels more natural and nourishing. Visit with them frequently in your mind (and physically, too if you can). Tell them about your day, about your life, about your wishes. And also ask them questions just like you would ask a friend.

+ **Make them an offering from time to time.** Offerings could look like sharing verbal gratitude for what you have learned from them, or it could look like building an altar either in your home or in the natural world and infusing it with your gratitude. I love to build mini-shrines when I am out hiking and offer them to my animal teachers.

+ **Most importantly, add this animal teacher to your growing list of personal resources and remember to relate with them as frequently as possible.** They can serve as an attachment figure for you—even if you don't know them in the flesh. Your relationship with them will create a consistent (and mutual) resource on your journey of remembering you are not separate and earning secure attachment. And just like plant allies and sacred places, you have many, many more animal teachers waiting to connect with you. Stay receptive and they will always find you whether in your waking or your dream life.

I had a client named Taylor who initially came to me for relief from chronic anxiety. A wife and part-time, stay-at-home mother of two young children, she shared with me that she felt overwhelmed by the daily pressures of her life. "I'm exhausted," she said. "I'm completely burned out, and I see no end in sight."

When I asked her how her anxiety has been showing up for her, she said, "I lie in bed at night with my heart nearly beating out of my chest and my mind just going crazy. I just know I forgot something important that I was supposed to do today, but I can't remember for the life of me what it was. I feel so uneasy most of the time and like no matter what, I am always doing things wrong." It was clear she felt like she was drowning and there were no boundaries around her time or energy. She was giving it all to her kids and her work, leaving nothing for herself.

During our first treatment, I noticed she had a large tattoo of a lion's head on her sacrum. With glowing golden eyes and a large mane, it was a beautiful tattoo. As I was doing some cupping on her low back to help her release tension and build up of stress hormones, I asked her the significance of this tattoo. Taylor told me a story from when she turned twenty-one: she quit her job, broke up with her high school sweetheart, paused college, and bought a one-way ticket to Costa Rica. From there, she ended up spending a year traveling solo around the world, visiting places such as Brazil, India, Vietnam, Alaska, and finally landing in Kenya. While in Kenya, she volunteered at a national park in exchange for room and board. While there, Taylor spent a month learning about and tracking a pride of lions who called the park home. She was able to check in on them nearly every day, watching them hunt, eat, play, and rest. She felt tenderized by the two lions who were leading and protecting their pride of over twenty lionesses. The lions played ever-so-gently with the cubs and yet became merciless when they felt their pride was under threat. Out of her entire year abroad, "my time with the lions," she said, "was the most life changing."

"When I returned home, I knew it wouldn't be long before I got swept back up in work and school responsibilities, so I decided to commemorate my trip with the lion tattoo. It hurt like hell getting it on my sacrum, no one warned me! It was like the needles were grinding into my bones. But it felt important to do at the time." She ended her story with, "I was so much more brave then. I can't imagine doing something like that now."

After her first acupuncture and cupping treatment, her anxiety was brought down to a more manageable level. I saw her for her second treatment a week later, and we continued our work to get her anxiety even more under control. We practiced plant breathing together on the treatment table using the plants hanging in the window, and I burned some mugwort (also called moxa or moxibustion) on her belly to ground her energy. (Mugwort is an herb used in healing practices in many places around the world that I also happen to have tattooed on my own body in honor of its sacredness).

After working on her belly, I asked Taylor if she could turn over so that I could do some acupuncture on her sacrum. As she turned over and I began working on her lower back, I was struck by her powerful tattoo once again. Here is this amazing woman, I thought, who has lived a courageous and fierce life. She has traveled the world solo, birthed, and is raising two children, and she is anxious about whether she is meeting her children's needs and appeasing her coworkers.

"Taylor," I began, "when was the last time you thought about those lions you spent time with in Kenya?"

"Oh, that feels like a lifetime ago," she chuckled.

I shared my observations with her. "Lions are the kings and lionesses the queens, they are the highest ranking predators living at the top of the food chain. They have to set boundaries; otherwise the lives of their pride are at stake. They also have to be present: when they are playing, they are playing—not worrying about the next thing. When they are protecting, they are protecting, and not worrying about what is coming next. What would it be like to embody some of this courageous lion energy in your life?" I asked.

"Gosh, I hadn't thought of that. But as you speak of it, I am remembering being with them and just how easy and simple things felt back then. They were either playing, resting, hunting, eating, or protecting. They weren't worrying about all the other things in between!" she laughed out loud. "I will think about it. Thanks for making that connection."

The following week Taylor showed up to her appointment excited to share with me that she went home after her last treatment with renewed energy. She broke out her photo albums from that trip and reminisced over the photos from Kenya. She even shared them—along with stories from her journey, with her eldest daughter for the first time. We talked about evoking and embodying the energy of the lion as an antidote for when she was feeling out of control, anxious, ashamed, and overwhelmed. Also, since her tattoo was on her back and therefore out of sight, she decided to print a picture of a lion so she could stay closer to its powerful medicine.

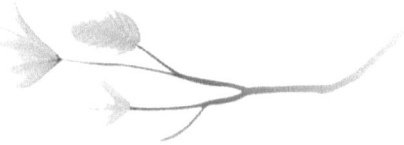

CHAPTER TWELVE:
CONNECTING WITH A HEALTHY ANCESTOR

ESTABLISHING A SACRED PLACE, discovering plant allies, and welcoming animals as teachers will support you in remembering your innate connection with the Earth and provide you with an enormous amount of resources. Step four, *connecting with a healthy ancestor* will amplify your sense of connection with other humans and serve by reminding you that while there may be trauma and hardship in your lineage, there is also wisdom, courage, and love you can tap into.

Just like relating with plants and animals, learning to relate with our human ancestors is an essential skill to remember. Blood ancestors are powerful beings to work with as our intergenerational limbic imprinting passes through our nervous systems, keeping us deeply connected with them (whether or not we choose it). If you are someone who feels a strong connection with your family and blood ancestors, that's something to be celebrated as it is quite rare these days. This step in the process of connecting with a healthy ancestor might be easier for you. Of course, all humans are our ancestors, even the ones not directly descended from our blood lineage.

In your journey of earning secure attachment with the Earth, I recommend strengthening your relationship with one other healthy human ancestor. I trust that you have at least one who continues to be a part of your life, whether or not it is conscious for you. This ancestor is likely dying to connect with you and let you know they are there and available for support. As your ancestor, they have access to an enormous amount of wisdom gained from many generations back that is specific to you and your lineage. This is the material that sets the foundation for your inner landscape, after all.

The healthy ancestor I am inviting you to connect with in the following practice will be a human who is no longer living. They will be someone who was stable before their passing, and since their passing, when you conjure them up in your mind and heart, you feel a sense of kinship, warmth, openness, and love. If you conjure them up in your mind and heart and instead feel chaos, coolness, scared, or as though they need *your* help, consider setting this relationship aside for the moment.

Perhaps as you were working on your genogram, you felt a resonance with one of your ancestors, or maybe while you were building out your family tree, there was someone whose life and story struck a chord with you. Or maybe there is an ancestor who your family speaks of with high regard, who you have always been curious about but never actually met. Regardless, choose someone healthy from your family lineage to work with during this process.

If, on the other hand, you are someone who struggles with your family relationships, feels disconnected from your blood lineage, or if you do not have access to information about your blood lineage, find a healthy human ancestor who is not directly related to you. Instead, find another human who you hold with high regard. Here are some examples of beings who have served the role of healthy ancestors for some of my students: a childhood neighbor, childhood schoolteacher, childhood guidance counselor, St. Brigid, Goddess Quan Yin, a Lakota Medicine Man, 14th Dalai Lama, father/mother archetypes, grandmother archetype White/Green Tara, Gaia, Hildegard of Bingen, and the Sage archetype. This process can be equally powerful even when not working with blood ancestors.

If it is possible, engage in this practice while in your sacred place:

1. **Find a healthy ancestor.** Choose a healthy ancestor from your family lineage or an archetype, a real or mythological god, goddess, or deity, a saint, or another human who you hold with high regard. If you have a picture of this being or have one of their belongings, consider placing it near you for this exercise.

2. **Ground yourself in your body and on the Earth.** Scan your body from head to toe, giving each part of your body a moment of your attention. Just notice your internal landscape, no judgment. Then, with your feet on the Earth, take a few deep plant breaths.

3. **Call in your supportive guides.** Once you feel mostly present and fairly grounded, I invite you to speak out loud and call in all those who support you. Call in animal and plant spirits who support you, call in God, Goddess, Gaia, whatever, or whoever you look to for guidance. When you feel their presence, move to the next step.

4. **Call your healthy ancestor into the space.** Close your eyes and imagine your healthy human ancestor is standing right in front of you. Notice what they look like, what they are wearing, not only clothes but also jewelry, their hairstyle, and other details. Are they taller than you, or shorter? Are they holding anything in their hands? Spend a moment appreciating them and showing gratitude for their presence in your space today.

5. **Notice your felt sense.** Feel in your body what it is like to have them near. Does it feel comforting? If it does not, for your own psychological safety, consider asking this being to step aside for now and choose another person to work with, starting over with the invitation. If it

feels comforting to have them present, keep going. Where do you notice the sensation in your body? In the upper half or lower half? In your torso or your limbs? Does this comfort bring warmth, coolness, movement, stillness, expansion, or contraction? Just notice.

6. **Gain permission.** Though they likely are already aware, go ahead and let them know why you called them here today. Share with them your intention of earning secure attachment with the Earth, repairing from attachment wounds, and/or building resources for yourself to use in your life. Let them know you consider them to be a healthy ancestor and that you would like to explore your connection with them. Ask them, "*are you open to this today?*" And simply be present in your body to "listen" for the answer whether you hear it, feel it, or see it. If you sense permission, keep going. If there is any hesitation or if you sense anything other than permission, then pause. Perhaps this ancestor needs more time, and you could return to this connection later. Or consider working with a different ancestor. As you are continuing to repair your relationship with your intuition, it is vital to listen and respond to the information you are receiving.

7. **Share some of your story.** Once you have their permission, go ahead and share with them a little about why you called on them, and what is weighing on you that you could use their help with. Speak from your heart but be pithy; share the headlines.

8. **Ask for their support.** Once you feel as though you have given them a good sense of what you could use their support with, consider asking them the following question: in what ways are you available for support? And simply be present in your body to "listen" for the answer whether you hear it, feel it, or see it. Sometimes ancestors will offer support that is nonverbal such as if you feel a change in your

body's felt sense or if suddenly a robin lands nearby. Others may say directly what they are available to offer. Listen with your *whole* body.

9. **Make an offering of gratitude.** Once you have a sense of how they can support you on your healing journey, ask them the following question, "*how can I show you my gratitude?*" Perhaps they would like for you to greet them each morning, or they would like for you to make them a plate of food during holiday meals. Perhaps they have a favorite herb they would like for you to burn or sprinkle on the ground. Ask them, and "listen" for an answer.

10. **Give thanks.** When you feel complete with your connection, give gratitude out loud to all the beings you invited in to support you during this invitation, including your ancestors and your supportive guides.

Now that you have found one of your healthy ancestors, nurture your relationship with them by connecting with them frequently, inviting them to journey through your day with you, asking them questions, and listening to their responses with your whole body. Keep a picture of them near you and on your altar to remind you of this person. Most importantly, add this healthy ancestor to your list of personal resources. Your relationship with them will create a consistent resource for you on your journey of earning secure attachment and they may very well become an attachment figure for you.

Sasha, a long-time student of mine developed an interest in her family history after attending a retreat with me. Growing up, Sasha was very close to her grandfather on her maternal side and even went to live with him on occasion during her parent's divorce. Her grandfather passed away a few years prior, and so she decided to try to connect with him as a healthy ancestor. Given the close bond she had with him before and during his passing, she felt comforted when she thought of him and anticipated that he would be healthy and available to connect with.

During the invitation to connect, Sasha placed a picture of her grandfather on a small table in front of her along with a note he had written her on her 30th birthday just before he passed that said, "So glad I got to be your grandfather in this life. There could not have been a greater gift. You are my sunshine, and I love you. Happy Birthday, Sash!" With these two items in front of her, Sasha closed her eyes and began conjuring her grandfather in her mind. Once she felt connected with him and could see him in her mind's eye, she reported feeling emotional, a mixture of excitement, tenderness, and also grief. She placed a hand over her heart and let herself cry for a moment. With his energetic presence, she also felt loved, warm, as well as a child-like sense of playfulness—a reprieve from the current onslaught of the weight of responsibilities in her life.

She asked him if he was available to be a healing resource for her to call upon when she needed his support. In her vision, he had tears in his eyes, and was overjoyed she asked. All he asked for in return was to purchase a pack of Marlboro cigarettes once a year in his honor (those were his favorite apparently). Sasha caught him up with details of her life over the last few years and shared with him the healing work she was doing. She could sense how very proud of her he was. Sasha now connects with her grandfather at least once every week, calling on him and his stable, loving presence to support her on her healing journey and in life's other big moments.

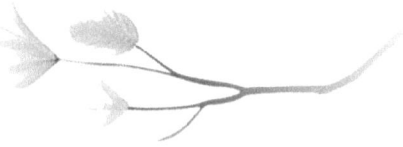

CHAPTER THIRTEEN:
ENTERING THE WILDERNESS

HUMANS HAVE BEEN LOOKING to their relationship with the Earth for many years for support in healing, visioning, guiding, and comfort. Earth has served as the *secure base* for humans across continents and continues to do so in communities that still honor their interdependent relationship with her.

I have spent years living with and working alongside the tribal communities found deep in the Himalayas of Nepal. Each community has a shaman, a medicine carrier who is known for their strong relationship with Mother Earth and her beings. These shamans frequently have one leg in each realm, traversing the Earth-based and Spirit-based states regularly and with a sense of everyday normalcy. When someone in the community is experiencing hardship or illness, they do not go see a doctor (many of these communities do not have access to traditional medical doctors); they go visit with their village's shaman. They trust the wisdom of the medicine carrier specifically *because* of their personal relationship with and deep connection to the Earth, her plants and animals. Frequently these medicine carriers have visions for their community that includes the natural world, such as needing to spend time where a certain wild animal dwells or consuming a specific plant so as to gain insight into a person's illness or condition, to find guidance in birthing, living, and in dying.

Historically, in many Earth-honoring communities around the world, there was a common rite of passage centered on this union with the natural world called a wilderness quest, wilderness solo, vision quest, vision fast, and other similar terms. (For the sake of neutrality, in this text I will refer to this general experience as a *wilderness solo*. Many of these other terms have been used by specific tribal communities with distinct rites that I have no authority to write about.) While the expression "rite of passage" was coined by Arnold Van Gennep, a Dutch-French-German ethnographer and folklorist, rites of passage can be found in traditional cultures all around the world. The wilderness solo, for example, was a rite of passage that was warranted for an individual in a community when transitions were taking place, and the bigger questions were being asked, such as, *"where do I belong?"* And, *"what am I doing here? What are my gifts?"*

A wilderness solo is exactly what you would imagine: time spent in the wilderness, solo (and often fasting). I've learned over the years as I've introduced this practice to many students that the first place they go in their psyches in response to hearing of time spent solo in the wilderness is *fear*. And that is completely natural—in fact, one could even say that is what gives way to the power in the practice itself. It is an experience that calls on you to be courageous, for without that, we don't have the opportunity to see ourselves so clearly, our strengths and our gifts. While working with and overcoming fear is a natural part of the experience, a wilderness solo also requires that you reduce or eliminate the daily onslaught of distractions so that you can actually hear yourself—your authentic inner voice—as well as to hear the voices of the Earth, the plants and the animals. This is a key element in remembering we are not separate.

Traditionally a wilderness solo would include an individual leaving the community for several days, frequently without food and also sometimes without water or shelter. Prior to leaving, there would be a ceremony held for the person who is going out solo that would enable the community to hold this individual's intention for their journey. The community would pray for her each day while she was out on the land. Some communities would light a fire when she left, tending it, visiting it frequently to pray, and keep it burning until she returned.

You may ask yourself, why are these immersions in the natural world considered to be so powerful and life changing? Because in that timeless space, you are reminded of your deep connection to and oneness with the Earth, and without distraction you can feel her unwavering presence. And after some time unwinding and shedding the layers of trauma held in your nervous system, you will feel yourself, too—your true, authentic nature. You will open your eyes and find yourself unquestionably tethered to the Earth, your original secure base. And with this tether in place, healing becomes not only possible but also becomes *unavoidable*.

As you are working to remember you are not separate, this practice of leaving the dominant culture for anywhere from a few hours to days at a time is vital. The longer you stay immersed in a culture that is not in alignment with your values, the more difficult it becomes to feel yourself and hear your authentic voice.

Crafting Your Wilderness Solo

While it is not practical for all of us to step away from our lives for several days—to sever from our families, our careers, and communities, and head solo into the wilderness—when it comes to healing from trauma and earning secure attachment, I cannot recommend it more.

There are many ways to craft a wilderness solo experience—even without leaving your house if that is what is needed. One option is to set aside one full day where you will enter a room in your house, undisturbed by people or technology, and have your solo experience there. You could extend that to more than one day if you desire. You could also do a full day in nature, where the boundary you set is to not be indoors or in a car for the bulk of the day. I do this style of solo more frequently throughout the year as I am able to more easily fit this in given family, student, and client needs. You could drive to one of your favorite wilderness places at sunrise and simply stay outdoors for the full day, returning to your car when the sun goes down. Think of it as being in a day or days-long ceremony.

What I have found to offer the most life-changing transformation—if you are able, is to carve out a minimum of three nights and three days where you can get out and into the natural world. I have found that day one and night one is a time to discharge and leave society behind. It is also usually a time to manage the fear and anxiety that comes with saying goodbye to society for a few days. Sometimes this particular step takes awhile as you wait for the vibrations to leave your nervous system. You don't have to do anything for this to happen. However, if you practice plant breathing as well as exploratory orienting at each leg of the journey, your nervous system will regulate much quicker. Then day two-night two is usually a time for entering into sacred space, your consciousness changes, and you will begin to feel your nervous system settle enough so that the natural world can start to envelop you (and not all the animals will be startled by your presence). And day three-night three seems to be when most of the magic happens. You have quieted your nervous system enough that you have become a part of the landscape and are finally spacious enough in your nervous system to receive the messages, guidance, and wisdom from the Earth and her beings regarding your intention. As Frank MacEowen, in *The Mist-Filled Path,* says, "We remove ourselves from the unnatural rhythms of the world, the more ancient rhythm of our Earth selves returns. This is nature's healing power on us and within us. For we are a part of nature."

Whichever arrangement speaks to you will be perfect. It is up to you to find what timeline and style of solo immersion works for you and your life. Ask yourself, where does that wild edge live in me? Where do I feel just a little nervous but also excited and still within my window of tolerance?

There are many safe ways to experience this, no matter your level of skill or ability. I, for one, host one or more wilderness solo opportunities each year through my healing center in the Rocky Mountains. There are also numerous other individuals, companies, and schools who offer these kinds of structured, immersive experiences, and a list of these programs can be found in the resources section of this book. I recommend working with a teacher and/or with a small group the first several times you go out solo into the wilderness, especially if you are fasting, because fasting can dramatically change your consciousness—sometimes so much so that you feel like you have taken hallucinogens. In that case, it is wildly important to have someone holding space for you and able to keep you physically safe. For a list of wilderness solo resources, see page 234.

As I'm sure you can see, the Earth provides a mirror for you. You must learn to engage with her, ask her the big questions, and then stand by and listen for her response. This relationship is essential because you *are* her. Just like a baby's nervous system becomes a replica of the mother's nervous system when she is born, you too, become a replica of the Earth and her system; you are, after all, living in her field. As you learn to enter the wilderness, whether physically or energetically, you must learn to trust your intuition as you interpret the language of the Earth. This language is different: it is slow and often (though not always) metaphorical. You must learn to make your implicit relationship with her *explicit*. If you want to heal, to find out where you belong, discover your innate resilience, and hear your most authentic voice, you have to start by reconnecting with the greatest resource who lives just under your feet, Mother Earth. This is the final step in remembering you are not separate.

The Wilderness Solo

While the parameters of rites differ amongst cultures, they generally contain a similar flow: preparation, severance, initiation, and integration.

Preparation

After having committed to a wilderness solo, the preparation naturally begins. This will include logistical planning and preparation of the psyche and soul— the terms of which might be completely unknown at this stage. Preparation includes intention setting and is perhaps the single most important step that turns essentially any practice into a *sacred practice*. The clearer you are with your intention, the more courageous and resilient you will be as you face your fears during your solo time.

Janet, a profoundly wise and deeply spiritual client of mine, had been diagnosed at age fifty-five with Crohn's, a chronic autoimmune disease affecting the lining of the intestines. The diagnosis came with some relief as she had been suffering for a long time without any answers. However, she understood that there was no cure for Crohn's, so she would have to learn to live with it, so this diagnosis also came with a degree of uncertainty.

After speaking with her doctor, Janet reached out to me asking if I could guide her from afar on a twenty-four-hour solo in her apartment. Janet had attended two group wilderness solo experiences with me in the past, and so she knew the wilderness solo requirements of camping and being out on the land would not be the wisest or most supportive choice given her current health challenges.

When we had our intention-setting meeting, Janet disclosed she wanted to set the intention of, "coming to terms with my diagnosis, grieving the loss of my former, more active role in society, and opening my heart to what is next."

She decided on a date for her to begin and started to prepare her mind and body for the experience.

As you start preparing for your journey, the following are some ideas to consider:

1. **What is your intention for this experience?** Get as clear about this as possible up front. Spend weeks or months if you have to. Your

intention will hold you throughout the entire experience and continue to give you something to fall back on when the doubt demon shows up (which she does for all of us). Write out your intention in your journal and/or share it with those who know you are stepping into this terrain. This intention setting is when the journey actually begins, after all.

Some of the intentions of past solo participants have been:

+ Questioning whether to leave a job, a relationship, or to pack up and move
+ Marking a unique moment in time such as before entering a PhD program, before marriage or a commitment ceremony, celebrating or grieving a birthday or anniversary
+ Calling in something important such as conception, a new career, a partner, or a new business
+ Holding some of life's bigger questions such as: What is my sexuality? What is my gender? What is my purpose? Where do I belong? What are *my* unique gifts?

Setting intentions are crucial. When I guide wilderness solos, I hold an intention-setting meeting with each participant. If you decide to go on a wilderness solo, I recommend doing the same for yourself and with your guide if you choose to have one.

2. **How will you structure your solo?** Will you find a teacher or a company to host your wilderness solo (I highly recommend this for your first time so that you can lean on the support of others who have done this before)? Or will you do some variation of a solo in your home or near your house? Decide and set these parameters.

3. **How long would you like your solo to last?** Think in terms of full days. If you feel panicky when you think about four days, perhaps that is slightly too long for you right now. See how you feel when you think about three days, two days, twenty-four hours, or a few hours one morning or afternoon.

4. **Which distractions would you like to remove?** People? Technology? Food? Shelter? Books? Recording equipment such as cameras and journals? Set these boundaries and stick to them, knowing full well that you will have a protesting part of you show up just before the big day and try to talk you out of it.

5. **Set a date and let the magic unfold.** In the days or weeks leading up to a wilderness solo, I find that the natural world automatically begins speaking to you. Animals or plants that you have never noticed before may suddenly show up. People may say things that just so happen to align with the intention you set. Be on the lookout and write these things down, as they are all a part of the magic of your journey.

Severance

Once you have prepared your body, psyche, and soul as much as you are able to, the next step is to leave the community, your comfort zone, and all that is familiar. This phase often involves severing from other comforts and distractions, too, such as food, family, and societal obligations. Severing also includes saying goodbye to who you are at the time of your departure, as you will not be the same upon your return. This phase can sometimes feel like a death and bring much grief (and also, at times—a feeling of liberation).

Now that you have set your date and begun preparing your mind and body, I recommend spending some time pondering the following:

1. **What will you need to let go of so that you can be fully present during your solo?** This could be something emotional such as anxiety, fear, expectations, negative thinking, etc. Or it could be something physical such as your phone, elaborate skin care and/or hair care routines, food (choosing to fast is common though not required during wilderness solos).

2. **Who and what are you leaving behind physically and emotionally?** It is important to identify the individuals who are important to you that you are leaving behind. You may want to let them know what you are doing, possibly say goodbye, and give them notice of your expected return date. This is especially true if you have children. You want them to know that you will be coming back for them.

3. **Explore anchors that you would like to use to symbolize the severance part of your wilderness solo.** Often during solo time, you enter into some unexpected mental states, and having anchors can be grounding. Sometimes students like to bring an object to represent what they are leaving behind to serve as an anchor for bringing them back (physically and emotionally). This could be a photograph of your loved ones, a journal, or a personal item of significance. I have had students bring items such as a piece of one of their children's clothing, a dog toy, a pine cone from a tree in their yard, or a wedding ring. If you are entering the wilderness for your solo, I recommend leaving this object at the edge of your sacred place or on an outdoor altar. Or, if you are having your solo in your home, you could leave this object just outside the door or on an indoor altar.

Initiation

During this phase, you will be in uncharted territory, with your intention serving as your guide. You will no longer be tethered to your old self, and yet you will also not yet be anchored in your new self. This is a liminal, threshold space where *anything can happen*. In fact, all things that do happen in this space are important and often meaningful, so they should be made note of.

As you near your initiation phase, you may want to think about the following:

1. **Explore ways that you would like to enact the start of this phase of your wilderness solo.** You may want to cross some sort of threshold. This could be as simple as a piece of string you step over or a circle of stones you enter. I have had students create thresholds out of a circle of trees that they stepped through or even a piece of clothing that they took off or put on to symbolize the entering of this phase.

2. **How will you structure your time?** This is probably the most asked question and also the hardest to answer. The purpose of the wilderness solo is to have unstructured time so that you can hear, see, feel yourself and your relationship with the Earth more deeply and authentically. However, if you are used to a highly structured life, this may in fact be the most terrifying aspect for you of the entire experience. Therefore, if this inquiry speaks to you and you feel you would be well suited (and far less anxious) to have a bit of structure, consider creating a loose schedule. As an idea, you could plan to hold a ceremony that honors your intention at sunrise, a meditation to connect with the plants and/or animals at the height of the day, or time spent exploring your senses at sunset.

3. **What will you do when you want to turn and run?** As someone who has participated in and hosted many wilderness solos, I still find myself wanting to leave and return home when I am in my initiation phase. I find it helpful to already anticipate this feeling showing up; stepping into new territory of the psyche can be scary, after all. Identifying

some of your resources from Chapter Two and calling on them to support you will be helpful. Also, bringing your intention back to the forefront each time you find yourself falling into a place of fear, anxiety, and doubt is supportive. Perhaps writing your intention on a piece of paper so you can read it like a mantra when you need to be reminded of why you chose to do this in the first place.

Here are a few additional tips to make the most of your time during your initiation:

✦ Remember to keep your list of personal resources near for when you need the extra support, if not in physical form, on a piece of paper or somehow symbolized in your landscape.

✦ Pay attention to what is happening in your body at all times. What are the sensations you are experiencing? Are they tied to any particular thoughts or emotions?

✦ Remember to breathe. If all you did was go out on the land and breathe for a few days, you would still come back a remarkably different human being than before you went out.

✦ Pay attention to what is happening all around you, especially signs from nature if you are outside. What plants, trees, or animals do you notice? What weather patterns or signs of the season do you notice?

✦ Pay attention to your senses. What do you see? What do you smell? What do you hear? What do you taste? What do you feel? If you get caught up in doubt or negative thinking—simply return to your senses and explore what information you are gathering from them at the present moment.

✦ Is there a particular emotion that you keep coming back to that needs to move through you? Where in your body does it live? Can you do some plant breathing and direct your inhalations to this place? This may help it to move.

Integration

When you have finished your solo time and are ready to return to the community, you will enter the integration phase. You will begin the process of unpacking *what happened out there*, making meaning, and incorporating all that you brought back with you. Even though entering the wilderness solo seems like an individual adventure—you go out not only for yourself but also for your people. Whatever gifts you return with are, therefore, gifts for the collective and are meant to be shared.

During your integration phase, consider the following:

1. **Move slowly.** When the time comes to return to society and interact with people once again, do it ever-so-slowly. Take your time, pause as much as you need to. I have even stopped my car every few miles when driving home after a solo, gotten out, sat on the Earth for a few minutes, and then continued on. This practice (or some variation of it) can support you in staying closely connected to your experience as you reenter the pace and stimulation of society.

2. **What will you do when you don't want to return?** Just like there is often a part that wants to turn and run in the beginning, there is also often a part that wants to stay on the land or in the room, feeling connected to all that happened for you. Again, knowing this part might be useful. Connect with your anchor(s), as these will serve to remind you of who and what you are returning to and why.

3. **Be mindful of stimulation.** Our world can be immensely overstimulating once you begin reentry. Be aware and intentional about your level of engagement, such as deciding when to turn on your phone, when to check email (and for how long), when and what kind of music to listen to, and when and what kind of television to watch. Your newfound nervous system field may not be able to tolerate the kind of stimulation you were used to before your solo.

4. **Hold your story close.** Before sharing your story with those in your life of *what happened to you out there,* get clear on it with yourself (of course, if you went out with a guide and/or a group, they will help you with this part). You don't want to lose any details or be persuaded by others as to which parts were meaningful and which parts were not, or what meaning to take away from your experience. Find those things out for yourself first, and then consider sharing and requesting feedback if that feels important.

5. **Extract the medicine.** When will you get to extract the medicine of your experience? It takes about a year for the complete wisdom of a wilderness solo to unfold. Go gently, go slowly, and keep paying attention during the year following. Check in with your intention and the medicine you brought back on day one, week one, month one, month three, month six, and year one after you return. I recommend journaling as you cross these thresholds.

6. **Make a commitment.** Consider making a commitment to yourself that will honor your intention for your wilderness solo and/or the newfound medicine that came from your experience. With commitments, it is helpful to be very specific. Examples of commitments some of my past participants have made after their wilderness solos are connecting daily with the Earth for at least ten minutes, having a

challenging but needed conversation with a loved one, writing in their journal once each week, handing in their notice at their job, going live with their business and officially offering their services to the world, as well as starting each day with meditation and prayer.

7. **What gift will you return with?** While it may appear a wilderness solo is done only for yourself and your personal gain—remember, you also do these things for your community and for collective healing. Our communities are, after all, only as strong and connected as the individuals who comprise them. When one person engages in healing, their healing impacts the entire community. So I ask you to ponder upon your return, *what is the gift from this journey that you now carry for your people?*

Kimberly, a longtime therapist and mentoring student of mine, decided (after years of going back and forth) to join me on a wilderness solo I was hosting for a group of women in the desert about fifty miles south of Moab, Utah. She was nervous about it because she had never spent a single night away from her two daughters, then aged four and seven. She also didn't have much experience camping, so she felt daunted by the idea of camping for seven days but most especially camping alone for three days and nights. Despite her fear and anxiety, she signed up for the women's wilderness solo and made the emotional and financial commitment.

After she committed, Kimberly and I had an intention-setting meeting. Kimberly shared her intentions for the trip, "I want to know myself again as Kimberly, not as a wife and not as a mother. Who am I when I am not playing these roles?" She also shared with me her fears about leaving her daughters for a week. "What if something happens to them and they cannot get in touch with me? What if something happens to me, and I cannot get in touch with them?"

Given her fears and lack of camping experience, Kimberly decided to structure her wilderness solo in the following ways:

+ *She wanted to have her tent and all of her belongings with her during her solo time.*

+ *She did not want to fast but would instead simplify her meals during her solo time.*

+ *She wanted to find a sacred place within view of my tent (and our base camp) so that she felt safe while on her solo time.*

+ *She wanted to call her daughters the night before she left for her three day and night solo and also the morning of her return.*

+ *The anchors she brought with her were a family picture of her husband and daughters as well as a small bouquet from her garden, wrapped together in twine (Kimberly is an avid gardener).*

+ *She decided to bring a journal and a pen as she wanted to write to her former self each day (pre-wife, pre-mom self).*

+ *During her initiation time, she wanted to perform a cleansing ceremony with water from the nearby river and on her final night, hold a fire ceremony to let go of the "shoulds" she knew she had downloaded in her role as wife and mother.*

Kimberly honored her commitment to herself and her intention and attended the full seven-day wilderness experience with the three-day and night solo. With all the parameters she put into place beforehand, she mentioned feeling little to no anxiety on the night before she left for her solo time. And on the morning of her return to the group after being solo for three days, she did not feel the need to call her family and check in as she trusted that if they had not called the emergency phone, then all was truly well (though she called anyway because she made that commitment to her family and didn't want them to worry).

Over the course of two days, Kimberly—with the guidance and support of our group as well as the Earth and her beings, unpacked much of what she experienced while alone in the wilderness. She reported having deeply profound moments where she was able to separate herself from the voice in her head who is, "always worried about something." And in that separation, she said she could feel her own essence, "the Kimberly at my core." And she said, "Despite a big wave of anxiety my first night alone, I felt freer the next day and able to keep my codependent behaviors in check."

I witnessed Kimberly as she returned to her life with a newfound confidence in herself and with having committed to carving out intentional spaces in her busy life for being only with herself—her core-Kimberly self, and the Earth.

INTERLUDE

AS I LET GO of each and every thing that felt misaligned in my life, I felt deeper and deeper questions arise until I got to the one underneath them all: *where do I belong?* This question was to become my intention, my North Star.

If I didn't belong in my family, in my partnership, or with my colleagues, where did I belong? If I didn't belong in my career or my community, where did I belong? It wasn't long before I realized that the medicine I most needed would not be found by asking other humans. I needed to go ask Mother Earth herself. It was time for an immersion in the deep wilderness, solo.

Now this would not be my first time heading alone into the mountains. Once after the ending of a long-term relationship I decided to go on a solo. Before I started graduate school and became a practitioner, I went on a solo. As I was calling for new love to enter my life, I went on a solo. After my first four-legged love, Orion passed away I went on a solo. And I've gone out on solo other times, too. I've fasted between twenty-four hours and four days, and even during a seven-day solo (though that one included one small meal each day). I have found that each solo brings its own kind of medicine; in some, you get the dose right then and there on the land, and in others, it takes days, weeks, or even an entire cycle of seasons for the medicine to reveal itself to you.

Two months after making the decision to return to the wilderness, I woke up in a tent on the land with one of my dear friends and teachers, Katie who I have been co-leading wilderness solos with for years. I knew she had the strength to hold the space for me that I needed, to face the territory of feeling separate, of not belonging, and to guide me straight back into the heart of myself. Knowing fear and anxiety were going to show up, she supported me through their arrival and pointed me, again and again, back to my intention.

Was I crazy for signing up for something like this at what felt like such a tumultuous time in my life? What if I completely lose my vision out there? What am I trying to prove? My anxious mind was calling to me...calling to me to turn around, to change my mind. To find some excuse and go home, back into my comfort zone. *But was it really comfortable? Or was it just familiar,* I wondered?

Somewhere between anxious and excited, I stepped out of my tent that morning, grabbing only my water jugs, a sleeping pad, and a tarp. I began my long, solo hike up the side of the mountain, taking my time as I had decided to begin fasting the night before and wanted to remain steady on my already shaky feet. As I made my way into the woods, I could not bring myself to look back at Katie, who I knew was going to stand there drumming for me long after I was out of sight—that was her thing. I knew if I did look back, I may not make it out. A part of me didn't want to go—this part of me was afraid.

I have noticed that committing to spending time alone in the wilderness will *always* bring up fear and anxiety, no matter how many times I've done it. I know this is a natural, human response and part of our attachment to life. However, I also know that if my curiosity and intention feel strong enough, I can override these feelings for an experience that is important at a soul-level (while also, of course, setting myself up safely out in the wilderness). This is why having an intention is so important; you can lean on it when things feel difficult.

When I reached the top of the mountain and found a sacred place, I could just barely hear her drumming for me in the valley. I dropped my things on the ground and laid down, looking up at the beautiful sky starting to turn light. Tears welled up in my eyes.

I noticed the lethargy, the anxiety, and also a little excitement, too about what I would experience in my time on the land. Just then, a hummingbird flew right in my face. It startled me, but the hummingbird just hovered, inches away—with its wings moving so quickly that they almost looked still. After our intimate exploration, the hummingbird flew away. I knew nothing about hummingbird medicine at the time but I was about to discover her magic over the next few days.

Now that I was present on the sacred land I was to call home for the next three days and nights, I decided I wanted to speak out loud my intention so that I could be heard and held by the land, the plants, and the animals present:

Mother Earth, I feel so lost. I feel separate. I do not know where I belong. I do not know who or where my people are.

Just then, a breeze picked up from the west. Rustling the trees, including the quaking aspen I was sitting under.

I don't want to create a life out of fear. And I don't want to feel alone anymore.

The tears filled my eyes, and a lump formed in my throat. Just then, the hummingbird came zipping around the bend of rocks, this time with her friend. They both paused again, inches from my face. They were so close I could feel the wind generated by their tiny wings. I had to laugh out loud as these birds were so light and playful when my energy felt so dark and serious.

Where do I belong, Mother Earth?

After some time processing, I decided to take a walk and get more familiar with the land. As I meandered, my heart was heavy with the question: *where do I belong?* The sun came out from behind the clouds. Walking gently through the woods, I noticed how much life was there; so many little wildflowers and insects and birds, many of which—despite living in the Rocky Mountains for some time—were unfamiliar to me. Perhaps it was the lack of calories or perhaps it was sheer boredom, so I decided to start saying "hello" to each of them. *Hello, bluebell. Hello, lupine. Hello, ant. Hello, hummingbird. Hello, dragonfly. Hello, aspen.* And the walk went on like that.

The day moved at a snail's pace. There is something about removing food from our lives (planning meals, prepping them, enjoying them, and cleaning them up) that frees up so much space. I noticed the sun was getting nearer to the other side of the valley, which meant that soon it would fall behind the mountain ridge and get dark.

For me, the hardest part of any wilderness solo is knowing that I would soon be alone on top of this mountain in total darkness. I was going to have to face my vulnerability—something our modern lives tend to shield us from with our homes, our fences, and our artificial lights. *Was I going to get any sleep?* I wondered. I knew there were mountain lions and bears all around, and letting go enough to slip into sleep was going to be hard.

Alas, that time came, and the sun was dropping fast, and so was the temperature. I grabbed a few more layers and decided to sit on my sleeping pad with my back to a tree. Once it was dark, it was d-a-r-k. No street lights or lights from civilization, only the faintest sliver of moonlight in the sky. I had a headlamp in case of emergencies, but I knew if I used it, once I turned it off, it would make seeing in the dark even harder. So as I sat there, my vision becoming more useless by the minute, I closed my eyes and used my other senses.

I was beyond tired but far too awake, sensing and tracking through my ears, my nose, and my belly to fall asleep. Plus, the first night on any wilderness solo always seems to highlight the incongruence between the vibrations in my own nervous system field and the vibrations of the land. All the anxiety and feelings of separation I carry around with me in my life become wildly apparent when I am in a natural environment. Thankfully, my nervous system naturally begins to recalibrate after the first twenty-four hours or so of being undisturbed in a natural place.

In my anxiety, I sat up most of the night, leaning against a tall ponderosa pine. Though I must have fallen asleep just before sunrise because I awoke—sitting upright, neck stiff from hours with no movement. *I made it through the first night.*

I will be honest, though, and tell you that I felt rough: tired, slow, and a bit fragile—both physically and emotionally. But I wasn't as hungry as the day before, and I could sense the anxiety and feelings of separation I brought with me into the wilderness beginning to shift. I could feel myself *arriving* on the land—and more than just my physical body.

As the sun was coming up, I headed over to what was soon to become my favorite place to sit, just beneath the aspen trees on a rocky outcropping facing the east. The east, I know from studying Taoism and spending time with Indigenous, Earth-honoring communities, represents the energy of birth, newness, growth, and new-chapter-kind-of-energy. *And I was so ready for that.* I could feel how stuck and incongruent things were in my life and in my body.

With the warm sun covering me from head to toe, I sat back and drank it in. I pulled it deep into my body using my breath. Closing my eyes, I sank into the simplicity of the moment. I could feel the possibility of this new day like an effervescence in my veins. Placing my hand over my heart, I touched back in with my intention: *where do I belong*? I asked again out loud while gazing at the semi-dark horizon.

I'm not sure if it was the magic of the sunrise or the lack of food, but seeing the sun come up from the horizon that morning brought tears to my eyes. I felt both the awe of this new day and also a heaviness in my chest, reminiscent of grief. Grief and awe, I know, often sit side by side with one another, and our capacity for one is frequently matched by our capacity for the other.

The day went on slowly and rhythmically: moments of grief broken up by visits with the hummingbird, gentle wandering through the forest saying hello to the flowers and insects, naps, and continuing to ask: *where do I belong?*

That evening I was beyond tired. I hadn't had food for more than fifty hours—only water. And I could tell how different my body felt. On the one hand, my body felt fragile, wobbly, and delicate. But on the other hand, I was feeling more and more like myself inside. The layers were peeling back; the influence of the culture was getting weaker. My anxiety was lessening, and that was bringing more energy into my body. The landscape, its rhythms, and beings were becoming more familiar and therefore more comfortable. I opened up my sleeping pad on the ground once again and laid down under the stars. *Where do I belong?* I asked the night sky. But in my tiredness, I fell right to sleep without time to listen for an answer.

Some time later, I awoke suddenly to unusual sounds, the sounds we all fear while alone at night in the middle of the woods, the cracking of leaves and twigs on the forest floor as though someone or something was walking nearby. It was pitch black, but my senses opened up like a giant galaxy inside of me—assessing the threat. I wanted to sit up to orient myself to the threat, but I also didn't want to make a peep or move a muscle. So I laid there still, but tracking with my entire body. *What was out there,* I wondered?

Just then, I not only heard but felt the gust of a giant whoosh in the air. I knew for certain it was a large bird. This bird whooshed again, only feet from my head, going the other direction this time. It wasn't long before I heard the classic four hoots and knew it was a great horned owl. My instinct told me that the owl was not happy I was there; it seemed to be protecting something.

My question of belonging arose. *I don't belong here,* I thought. The owl doesn't want me here. She is trying to scare me away. But it's pitch black, and there is nothing I can do but lie here helplessly at her mercy. *I'm not here to hurt you,* I tried telling her. *I am here to listen.*

There was that familiar pang of grief again in my chest mixed with a sprinkling of feeling rejected. I wanted to cry. I felt the residue of old, unhealed traumas coming up: the trauma of not belonging, of not being wanted.

The owl whooshed so many times, this way and that way. It sounded like she was circling around me, landing in a nearby tree, and then diving and whooshing again. It felt like she was only feet from my head at times. She would let out this screeching sound when she got near that made my heart skip a beat and sent chills up my spine; a seemingly natural reaction for an owl who is feeling threatened.

With nothing to do but lay there in the dark and be still while the owl enacted her territorial dance, I could feel the sensations in my body so clearly—the sensations that come with the story that *I do not belong*. I knew, though wildly uncomfortable, with nothing else to occupy me, this experience with the owl was important. My heart beat hard and fast and it was almost painful to take a full breath. My body vibrated as though I was floating. I felt heat rising up my spine and settling around my neck and jaw. Though I could hardly see anything, my eyes were wide open. My jaw was clenched, as were my shoulders. *Is this how I am living my life each day,* I wondered.

Witnessing this dance between the owl and my own sensations, bringing my awareness from inside of me to the outside and back in again, I could feel the sensations shifting and beginning to dissipate. The owl also began flying further and further down the valley, eventually disappearing, and soon after, the sky lightened. *I made it through another night.*

I must have nodded off for some time because I awoke to the heat of the sun, feeling as though it was scalding me through my sleeping bag. To see the light of day, I felt a mixture of relief and of sadness. I was relieved for some sleep, as it felt like it pushed a reset button on my nervous system—especially after all the processing from the day before. But I also felt sad that my presence was encroaching on the owl's territory. Yet to pack my things up and move places felt like an astronomical feat, given that I had now been without food for more than sixty hours.

I felt tenderized by the night. I could hear my hummingbird friend a little further down the valley and walked gently over to my spot on the rocky outcropping near the aspen trees, which had become my daily ritual. Like clockwork, the hummingbird returned, just inches from my face. Again, her playful presence brought with it a lightness that transferred into my being, and I couldn't help but chuckle a bit.

Though I felt weak in my body, my mind had shifted from the experience with the owl the night before. I was feeling more clear, open, and relaxed than I had in a very long time. Having worked my way up from the ground, I walked slowly and gently through the woods that cradled the exposed piece of land I had come to call home during my solo time. Perhaps I would find a place to move my home to that wouldn't disturb the owl. *Where do I belong*? I asked the landscape.

As I stepped into the forest, I noticed something new: bear scat. *That wasn't there the day before.* I kept walking, making my way around the perimeter of the mountaintop, and there was more bear scat—only forty or so feet from where I laid my head the night prior. I continued to make my way around the perimeter until I saw the unmistakably huge paw prints in the dirt; they were bear prints.

At that moment, it hit me like a brick wall—the owl wasn't trying to shoo me away! The owl was trying *to protect me by shooing the bear away.* In my weakened state, I was overcome with emotion. I cried, and I cried hard. I let the emotion wash over me. And I savored it with every ounce of my fragile being: the owl was an ally, and *she was protecting me.*

As someone who was frequently in the role of caregiver for others (family, clients, students, etc.), to feel that another being was trying to protect me was surprising, almost foreign. And yet, as it turned out, I wanted (needed) nothing more than that my whole life. To my delight, I was being cared for by this owl. She did not see me as an invader or as a threat, but rather as a part of her landscape. I was right where I needed to be. *That was where I belonged.*

Something shifted in me that day—something big. I didn't know it at the time, but I was repairing some of the damage done by my early childhood attachment trauma that led me to believe that I was separate and therefore did not belong here, there, or anywhere. This was huge. Suddenly I could feel possibility in my nervous system. I was beginning to understand that no matter where I found myself, *I belonged*—because I belonged to the Earth. I belonged just as much as the owl and the bear and the hummingbird. I belonged just as much as the ponderosa pine and the aspen. *I belonged to the Earth.* My nervous system was repatterning.

That night on the land, I slept like a baby knowing the owl was watching over me. I could hear her hooting in the distance, the sound ricocheting off the sides of the valley. I felt at ease, like I hadn't in a very long time. *I wasn't separate. I wasn't alone.*

I awoke gently the next morning to the sounds of drumming in the distance. It was my teacher calling me back. Her rhythmic beating nearly matched the beating of my heart. Sunlight was just beginning to sparkle on the horizon. My lips were cracked and dry. My hair was matted underneath my hat. I hadn't had a meal in three days and nights—only water and sunlight, yet I felt more satiated than I had in years. I could feel my heart beating hard in my chest, but I was not anxious—this was *my life force*. I could feel myself for the first time in a long time. I could *hear my inner voice clearly* for the first time in a long time. This was the very tending that I needed. I had found belonging. I had come home.

It was time to pack up my things and head back—slowly, gently down the mountain. I laughed and cried the whole way down, one foot in front of the other, feeling the presence of the owl right behind me.

FOR ME TO MAINTAIN this deep connection with myself and in relationship with the Earth, I have committed to welcoming some version of a wilderness solo each year of my life. No matter how it looks, the intention is always the same: to nurture my connection with the Earth and all her beings. It does not always feel convenient; however, each time I return from these experiences, I feel more and more rooted in myself, in my body, and in the Earth. Each time I go out, I come back feeling less separate, with more allies, and with an unshakeable sense of belonging.

It feels important to mention that entering the wilderness or even being alone for a long period is not the only way to have a profound change of consciousness and to heal the wounds of separation. Another powerful way is to travel to another country and immerse yourself in a completely different culture. This can be done on a family trip, a vacation, a service trip, or even a work trip if you set a clear enough intention. You can simply use these same parameters that you set for a wilderness solo (preparation, severance, initiation, and integration) and enact them to turn the trip into a rite of passage experience. For example, as part of my nonprofit, Inner Ocean Empowerment Project, we visit our communities in India, Nepal, Thailand, and/or Burma annually, and we structure our trips in this way. The result is that these experiences become—not just an international trip, they become life-changing spiritual experiences. If you feel called to learn more or to join in an experience like this, please visit our website for opportunities at www.inneroceanempowermentproject.org/volunteer.

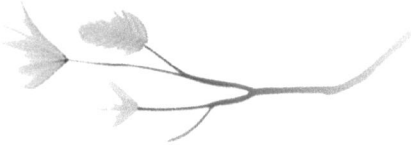

MAKING MEDICINE
WITH YOUR LIFE

"It is not enough to weep for our lost landscapes, we have to put
our hands in the Earth to make ourselves whole again. Even a
wounded world is feeding us. Even a wounded world holds us,
giving us moments of wonder and joy. I choose joy over despair.
Not because I have my head in the sand, but because joy is
what the Earth gives me daily and I must return the gift."

—Robin Wall Kimmerer

OUR HISTORIES—while they are wrought with the challenges of our ancestors, are simultaneously chock full of medicine for us. Your ancestors survived after all—the wars, the famines, the diseases, the persecution. Therefore, your lineage carries within it not only the residue of trauma but also the medicines of wisdom, courage, joy, and resilience.

There is a growing body of research on the opportunities to *make medicine* with the challenges in our lives called *Post-Traumatic Growth* (PTG). In the mid-1990s, psychologists Richard Tedeschi, PhD, and Lawrence Calhoun,

PhD, proposed a theory that positive transformation is not only possible after a traumatic experience but also fairly common, *if we're paying attention*. Some of the biggest themes they are seeing in the field of PTG are:

+ a new appreciation for life
+ a more optimistic perspective
+ seeing new possibilities
+ increase in personal strength (*I know I can handle this*)
+ new and deeper connections with others
+ a change in spiritual beliefs.

These transformations have led to a significant number of people, who have experienced trauma, going on to write books, become teachers, leaders, and healers, speak publicly about their experiences, start charities, and more. The generous gift of sharing their unfiltered stories reduces shame and increases healing opportunities for us all. Their ability to explore, understand, and ultimately to *make medicine from their lives*, holds within it the possibility for us all to find greater meaning and deeper healing on our own journeys.

As an herbalist who frequently makes medicine out of plants, I know that plants don't simply hand over their medicine. You can't swallow a piece of licorice root and obtain the benefits this incredible plant has to offer. You must create an optimal environment for licorice to release its powerful medicine. For example, if you pour boiling hot water onto the leaves of many raw plants, they will seize and develop scars, retaining their medicine inside thick plant scar tissue. However, if you allow them to get used to the hot water by slowly bringing them to a boil on the stove, they will open up like a spring flower and offer all the medicine they have to give.

We, humans, are no different. We cannot be expected to see or understand, let alone to share our medicine with the world, when the needs of our inner landscape are not being met. We need to be in relationship with the plants, the animals, the Earth, and to experience healthy attachment. Therefore, we must learn to create the kind of environment that meets our needs, creating a sustained felt sense of deep nourishment. Only then will our medicine become available. The question I hold for you now is this: what is the optimal environment for you to begin living your medicine into the world?

It's important to think of your medicine—not as a separate force in the Universe but rather as a part of the larger matrix of the world. In fact, if it weren't for others, there would be no reason to make medicine with your life because there would be no one to share it with. An evolved sense of belonging comes, after all, only when we feel we can contribute to the wellbeing of something or someone outside of ourselves. Therefore, one vital aspect of creating an attuned, nourishing, optimal environment must include welcoming other healthy humans into your world because healthy humans *can actually help you heal*. As you are already aware, we humans, have evolved in community and while times have certainly changed, our need for other humans has not.

With so much trauma centered around relationships with humans, it can become easy to think that humans are dangerous and should be held at arm's length. It is true, some humans are so traumatized and without access to resources to process and tend to their trauma that they can be very challenging to relate with. However, it is important to remember that *all challenging behavior comes from trauma*. The more unhealed trauma someone has living in their nervous system, the more braced, more rigid, more full of defenses, i.e., the more safety they are seeking inside themselves. And yet, underneath even the most perplexing, antisocial, and even aggressive behaviors, *we are all still wired for connection*.

There are many rewards to reap from having authentic, long-lasting relationships with other healthy humans. For one, healthy humans can provide what are called *corrective emotional experiences (CEE),* a term first coined in 1946 by psychoanalysts Franz Gabriel Alexander and Thomas Morton French. This describes the healing experience of being with another healthy, attuned human in such a way that it disproves some of the early patterning you experienced with unhealthy, unattuned humans. For example, if you learned early on that sharing your true feelings led to being criticized, having a healthy human in your life could now provide the opportunity to share your true feelings and be offered presence and compassion instead of criticism. This CEE can serve to repattern some of those painful, early lessons learned from communicating honestly with other humans. With this experience, our shame can transform and we can begin to create more authentic connections in our lives.

In addition, according to the field of interpersonal neurobiology, there are significant, measurable, healthy changes that occur in our brains and in our nervous systems when we are having positive interactions with other human beings (1). This includes the development of new neurons and new neuronal pathways leading to transforming even the most deep-seated trauma states. According to leading trauma researcher and author Bessel van der Kolk, MD, "Being able to feel safe with other people is probably the single most important aspect of mental health; safe connections are fundamental to meaningful and satisfying lives." You may already be aware of this benefit if you have humans in your life who are safe and supportive such as close, nurturing friendships, a solid therapist, an attuned and gentle acupuncturist, or a trustworthy bodyworker.

Furthermore, healthy humans can also support you by *co-regulating* your nervous system. Co-regulation is the process through which humans develop the ability to soothe and manage distressing emotions and sensations by connecting with fellow nurturing, safe, and reliable humans. What this means is that when your nervous system is in an unhealthy state, you can literally *vibe* off of a nearby healthy nervous system as a means to come back into balance more quickly than if you were trying to regulate alone. And when it comes to tending our unhealed trauma responses, the ability to co-regulate can open a whole new world of safety, joy, and connection.

We also need healthy humans so that we can have healthy physical contact. Is it any wonder that when we are touched by other humans, we gain access to oxytocin, the "love hormone," that lifts our mood and supports us in greater attachment to ourselves, our bodies, other humans, and to life itself (2)?

Finding healthy humans to have safe physical contact with provides another layer of healing for our nervous systems. If you do not have a partner, friends, or family who can support this aspect of your healing, consider finding a trustworthy practitioner who you can see regularly, such as a massage therapist, acupuncturist, or other attuned, hands-on practitioner.

Finally, establishing solid relationships with other healthy humans also enables them to serve as a secure base for you on your healing journey. In fact, research shows that if you developed an insecure attachment style during childhood, all it takes is one, single, healthy, consistent relationship to earn secure attachment (3). Of course, one challenging thing about learning to relate authentically with other humans is that it will often trigger your own attachment wounding. Though knowing this is likely coming, communicating about it, and setting yourself up with supportive resources can be helpful as you are approaching this terrain.

As you can see, healthy relationships with humans are critical as they provide safety, assurance, companionship, co-regulation, opportunities to repair from past wounding, proper mirror neuron development, new neuron development, not to mention access to creativity, sexuality, and play. They can remind us daily that *we are not separate.* Yet sustaining them does require skill, and for many of us, our relational skills fall short in large part because they were not modeled for us as children. Because this skill is vital, I am including several resources on creating and sustaining healthy, long-lasting relationships page 235.

While boundaries and recognition of separateness are important at specific times during our healing journey, ultimately we cannot heal alone. We all must work to heal together, *in tandem.* We need to involve others in our healing journey; the plants, the animals, the Earth, and our fellow humans. This is where the most impactful and sustainable healing happens. And the beautiful thing is that *because we are not separate*, when we begin to heal, we inevitably begin to see the impact our healing has on the world around us. It is truly a win-win.

Our shared human need to maintain a relationship with the Earth and her rhythms and beings isn't simply romantic, *it is life-saving*. So when you sense that traumatized, yet-familiar nervous system patterning and its messages of separation and shame beginning to creep back into your being, go to the Earth. Sit with her in one of your sacred places. Breathe with her plants. Witness her majestic creation using the power of your incredible sensory system. Talk to her, and then remember to stay long enough to listen—*really* listen.

EIGHTEEN MONTHS, five doctors, fifteen experimental injections, and in the end—surgery—and my vision finally started to come back. While I will always be at risk of losing sight again in my left eye, I could lose sight in both eyes if my life returns to the same level of stress as it once housed before. There is permanent damage in my vision in the form of scar tissue that light bounces off of from time to time—reminding me that even though I have come so far, I still have and always will have parts of me that need tending. And when the bouncing light catches my attention, I use it as a gentle reminder to pause, take a deep breath, and to remember: I too, am not separate, I belong here, and this world needs me. May you find your own reminders that continue to bring you back home.

Come find me, sit in circle with me or lay upon my treatment table. I would be honored to be a part of your healing journey. When the time is right, I hope you will let the world in, and let us see and experience the medicine you came here to offer us. And remember, always remember: you are not separate, you belong here, and *this world needs you.*

With deep love and courage,

Mindi

END NOTES

Introduction

1. White, M.P., Alcock, I., Grellier, J. *et al.,* "Spending at least 120 minutes a week in nature is associated with good health and wellbeing," *Sci Rep* 9, 2002, 7730, https://doi.org/10.1038/s41598-019-44097-3

2. Lee MJ, Oh W, Jang JS, Lee JY, "Horticulture-related activities significantly reduce stress levels and salivary cortisol concentration of maladjusted elementary school children," *Complementary Therapies in Medicine*, 2018, Apr 37:172-177, doi: 10.1016/j.ctim.2018.01.004. Epub 2018 Jan 6. PMID: 29609930.

3. Thoma MV, Rohleder N, Rohner SL, "Clinical Ecopsychology: The Mental Health Impacts and Underlying Pathways of the Climate and Environmental Crisis," *Front Psychiatry*, 2021 May 21;12:675936. doi: 10.3389/fpsyt.2021.675936. PMID: 34093283; PMCID: PMC8175799.

Chapter 1

1. Hannah Ritchie and Max Roser, "Forests and Deforestation." Published online at *OurWorldInData.org*, 2021, Retrieved from: https://ourworldindata.org/forests-and-deforestation

2. Partnership for Solutions, "Chronic Conditions: Making the Case for Ongoing Care,". 2002, Baltimore, MD

3. Ringel, S., "Developing the Capacity for Reflective Functioning Through an Intersubjective Process," *Clin Soc Work* J 39, 61–67 (2011). https://doi.org/10.1007/s10615-009-0246-9 Published 29 November 2009 Issue Date March 2011

4. Descilo T, Vedamurtachar A, Gerbarg PL, Nagaraja D, Gangadhar BN, Damodaran B, Adelson B, Braslow LH, Marcus S, Brown RP, "Effects of a yoga breath intervention alone and in combination with an exposure therapy for post-traumatic stress disorder and depression in survivors of the 2004 South-East Asia tsunami," *Acta Psychiatr Scand*, 2010 Apr;121(4):289-300. doi: 10.1111/j.1600-0447.2009.01466.x. Epub 2009 Aug 19. PMID: 19694633.

Chapter 2

1. "How Trauma Can Affect Your Window of Tolerance," The National Institute for the Clinical Application of Behavior Medicine

2. Suniya S. Luthar, Chris C. Sexton, "The High Price of Affluence," *Advances in Child Development and Behavior,* Volume 32, 2004, Pages 125-162, https://doi.org/10.1016/S0065-2407(04)80006-5

Chapter 4

1. David B Yaden, Matthew W Johnson, Roland R Griffiths, Manoj K Doss, Albert Garcia-Romeu, Sandeep Nayak, Natalie Gukasyan, Brian N Mathur, Frederick S Barrett, "Psychedelics and Consciousness: Distinctions, Demarcations, and Opportunities," *International Journal of Neuropsychopharmacology*, Volume 24, Issue 8, August 2021, Pages 615–623, https://doi.org/10.1093/ijnp/pyab026

2. Ben Sessa, "PTSD: From novel pathophysiology to innovative therapeutics," *Neuroscience Letters*, Volume 649, 2017, Pages 176-180, ISSN 0304-3940, https://doi.org/10.1016/j.neulet.2016.07.004.

Chapter 5

1. John Bowlby, *Attachment and Loss Volume One* (New York City: Basic Books, 1969)

2. https://www.who.int/teams/social-determinants-of-health/parenting-for-lifelong-health/infants

3. Tonetti-Vladimirova E, "The Limbic Imprint." Archived from the original on December 3, 2013. Retrieved 9 October 2013.

4. Tronick, E., "The Inherent Stress of Normal Daily Life and Social Interaction Leads to the Development of Coping and Resilience, and Variation in Resilience in Infants and Young Children," *Annals of the New York Academy of Sciences*, 2006, 1094: 83-104. https://doi.org/10.1196/annals.1376.008

5. John Bowlby and Mary Ainsworth, "The Origins of Attachment Theory" *Developmental Psychology*, Bretherton I 1992, 28 (5):

759–775. doi:10.1037/0012-1649.28.5.759

Chapter 6

1. Efrat Barel, University of Haifa and the Max Stern Academic
   College of Emek Yezreel; Marinus H. Van IJzendoorn, Leiden
   University; Abraham Sagi-Schwartz, University of Haifa; Marian
   J. Bakermans-Kranenburg, Leiden University, "Surviving the
   Holocaust: A Meta-Analysis of the Long-Term Sequelae of a
   Genocide," *Psychological Bulletin*, Vol. 136, No. 5.

Chapter 8

1. Peoples HC, Duda P, Marlowe FW, *Hunter-Gatherers and the
   Origins of Religion*, Hum Nat. 2016 Sep;27(3):261-82. doi:
   10.1007/s12110-016-9260-0. PMID: 27154194; PMCID:
   PMC4958132.

Chapter 9

1. Bethany Ojalehto Mays, Rebecca Seligman, Douglas L. Medin,
   "Cognition Beyond the Human: Cognitive Psychology and
   the New Animism," First published: 29 April 2020 https://doi.
   org/10.1111/etho.12264

Afterword

1. Siegel, Daniel J, MD, "An Interpersonal Neurobiology Approach to
   Psychotherapy," *Psychiatric Annals*, Thorofare Vol. 36, Iss. 4, (Apr
   2006): 248–256.

2. Wilhelm, F. H., Kochar, A. S., Roth, W. T., & Gross, J. J., "Social
   anxiety and response to touch: Incongruence between self-evalua-
   tive and physiological reactions," *Biological Psychology*, (2001) 58,
   181–202.

3. Shorey, Hal, PhD, "Finding A Secure Base and Rewiring Your Personality," Posted July 21, 2015, https://www.psychologytoday.com/us/blog/the-freedom-change/201507/finding-secure-base-and-rewiring-your-personality

RESOURCES

Working With Me

I offer one on one work, as well as group work. I support everyone from those in the beginning stages of their healing journey all the way through more advanced legs of the journey. I also work with and mentor practitioners of both holistic and allopathic healing arts. I offer online self-paced and live courses as well as live and in-person courses. I do my best to keep this information up to date on my site. In addition to joining me for a workshop or retreat, please consider signing up for my monthly newsletter where you will receive first access to any new offerings or opportunities to work together. Please visit: mindikcounts.com/offerings for a complete list of offerings.

Ancestry

+ 23andme.com

+ Ancestry.com

+ LivingDNA.com

BIPOC Ancestry

+ Africanancestry.com

+ Powell, Kimberly. "African American Family History Step By Step." ThoughtCo, Aug. 28, 2020, thoughtco.com/african-american-family-history-1421639.

+ https://www.familysearch.org/en/wiki/African_American_Genealogy

Native Land Acknowledgment Map

+ https://native-land.ca

Ancestral Healing Work

+ *Ancestral Medicine: Rituals for Personal and Family Healing* by Daniel Foor, PhD

+ *Healing Ancestral Karma: Free Yourself from Unhealthy Family Patterns* by Dr. Steven Farmer

+ *Deep Liberation: Shamanic Tools for Reclaiming Wholeness in a Culture of* Trauma by Langston Kahn

Wilderness Immersion Programs

+ Mindi K. Counts, MA, LAc. https://www.mindikcounts.com/offerings/

+ Animas Valley Institute https://www.animas.org

✦ Somatic Wilderness Therapy Institute
https://www.wildernesstherapyinstitute.com

Parenting Resources

✦ *Parenting from the Inside Out: How a Deeper Self-Understanding Can Help You Raise Children Who Thrive* by Daniel J. Siegel, M.D. & Mary Hartzell, M.Ed.

✦ *Last Child in the Woods: Saving Our Children from Nature-Deficit Disorder* by Richard Louv

✦ *The Whole Brain Child: Twelve Revolutionary Strategies to Nurture Your Child's Developing Mind* by Daniel J. Siegel, M.D., and Tina Payne Bryson, Ph.D.

✦ *The Conscious Parent: Transforming Ourselves, Empowering Our Children* by Shefali Tsabary

Relationship Resources

✦ *Attached: The New Science of Adult Attachment and How It Can Help You Find—and Keep—Love* by Amir Levine and Rachel Heller

✦ *Belong: Find Your People, Create Community, and Live a More Connected Life* by Radha Agrawal

✦ *Conscious Loving: The Journey to Co-Commitment* by Gay Hendricks, Ph.D and Kathlyn Hendricks, Ph.D

✦ *Nonviolent Communication: A Language of Compassion* by Marshall Rosenberg

+ *The Art of Showing Up: How to Be There for Yourself and Your People* by Rachel Wilkerson Miller

+ *The Five Love Languages: The Secret to Love That Lasts* by Dr. Gary Chapman